ADAPTING TO A NEW PLACE CALLED HOME

ADAPTING TO A NEW PLACE CALLED HOME

The Coptic Immigration Experience in the United States of America

Bishop Youssef
Coptic Orthodox Diocese of the Southern United States of America

Adapting to a New Place Called Home: The Coptic Immigration Experience in the United States of America

Copyright © 2016 His Grace Bishop Youssef.

All rights reserved.

Designed & Published by:
St. Mary & St. Moses Abbey Press
101 S. Vista Dr., Sandia, TX 78383
stmabbeypress.com

Printed in the United States of America

All Scripture quotations, unless otherwise indicated, are taken from the New King James Version® Copyright © 1982 by Thomas Nelson, Inc. Used by permission. All rights reserved.

Library of Congress Control Number: 2015906544

His Holiness Pope Tawadros II
118th Pope and Patriarch of the
Church of Alexandria and
the See of St. Mark

Contents

Introduction		1
Chapter 1	The Coptic Heritage	5
Chapter 2	The Early Years of Copts Immigrating to America	9
Chapter 3	Reflections from the First Generation of Immigrants	15
Chapter 4	How Copts Adapted to the New Culture	65
Chapter 5	Stages of Adaptation	71
Chapter 6	Additional Challenges Facing Immigrants	83
Chapter 7	Adaptation and Spiritualty	89
Chapter 8	The Copts Today in America	97
Chapter 9	Beyond the Home Stage: Trasnforming American Culture	105
Chapter 10	The Future for American-Copts & Coptic-Americans	111
Chapter 11	American Copts in the Future of the Coptic Church of Alexandria in the United States	115

Introduction

> "Go therefore and make disciples of all the nations, baptizing them in the name of the Father and of the Son and of the Holy Spirit, teaching them to observe all things that I have commanded you; and lo, I am with you always, even to the end of the age. Amen."
>
> Matthew 28:19-20

Migration and expeditions are not uncommon topographies for Christians. The Holy Scripture invites us to learn about the sundry dwellings and relocations of persons called by God to journey to diverse geographic regions—tranquil and hostile alike. In every scenario, God had a special vision to redeem lost souls and to reveal a distinct mission for His servants—His ambassadors on earth. In the Old Testament, we learn of the travels of Abraham, Joseph, Moses, Jeremiah, Jonah, Ruth, and many others. Some trekked willingly and others were reluctant. The New Testament introduces us to the extensive trips and passages of St. Paul and the other apostles who launched Christianity throughout the world. Even until this day, their work continues in their successors, the new generations of the traditional apostolic leadership, the believers, and through the vast churches established all around the world.

The Coptic Orthodox heritage is distinctly filled with spiritual modules, cultural thresholds, and proliferated wisdom extricated from the teachings of the Holy Scripture, the early Church Fathers, Holy Tradition, and lessons gleaned from the journey through life from generation to generation. In the late 1950's and early 1960's, a new thought emerged and flourished swiftly—emigration. Though some considered other nearby Middle Eastern countries for reasons of familiarity, North America, Australia, and Europe became the main focus of travel and the pursuit of a new life beyond the Egyptian borders.

This book takes us through the historic voyage that began a little more than a half century ago. It is an expedition of perseverance, laborious efforts, struggles, accomplishments, and triumph. The journey continues with future hopes of a faithful people rooted in an ancient but predominantly spiritual culture into new frontiers. The United States of America has become the new home for many Coptic immigrants. Pivotal experiences helped shape the Coptic-American experience and integrate it into the tapestry of holistic

American culture, but without losing its unique character, tradition, and legacy.

Today, the Coptic Orthodox diaspora is rapidly growing. Diligence and determination in evangelism efforts helped establish churches in South America, Mexico, the Caribbean Islands, Central America, and Asia. The populations in these countries are predominately of their ethnic culture rather than of Egyptian origins. Evangelistic from its inception, the Coptic Orthodox Church has been given new wings for new times to fulfill the Great Commission.[1]

Bishop Youssef

Bishop, Coptic Orthodox Diocese of the Southern United States of America

---

[1] Matthew 28:19-20

Chapter 1

THE COPTIC HERITAGE

"Blessed is Egypt My people."
Isaiah 19:25

The ancient Egyptian culture was compromised of a people remarkably fascinated by God and ready to worship a deity. They struggled for many centuries in pagan indulgences, but painstakingly in an awkward paradox, they searched for a god. Their intense motivation in the afterlife is evinced in their enduring legacies of monuments and pyramids. Akhenaton, the reigning Pharaoh from about 1350–1333 B.C., actually came close when he believed that God is one. Thus, monotheism entered the Egyptian intellect, but after the death of Akhenaton, the pagan Egyptians returned to their former polytheistic beliefs. Perhaps it was their zeal and interest in searching for god, though the true God was not yet revealed to them, that they caught His attention—the only one God who knows and searches the hearts. This is reminiscent of St. Paul who was a persecutor of the Early Church, but the Lord valued his zeal and transformed the persecutor into a witness for Himself and an apostle and martyr. Thus, the Egyptians were transformed from pagans to steadfast and faithful Orthodox Christians.

Without a doubt, the summation of the deep spiritual relationship between the Copts and God is found in the most popular and commonly used verse that Egyptian Christians adoringly proclaim as an expression of their love and faith in God—"Blessed is Egypt My people" (Isaiah 19:25). This prophecy was made long before Christianity entered Egypt, although there were many signs and prophecies that would culminate in an extraordinary long-lasting blessing that Egypt would obtain as the only country beyond Israel-Palestine in which the Holy Family would settle.[2] Isaiah's prophetic words became the greatest substantial and underpinning foundation upon which

---

[2] Matthew Chapter 2

the Copts endured centuries of persecutions and martyrdom.

The entry of the Holy Family into Egypt began the fulfillment of many prophecies about Egypt and the Christian roots that would be deeply placed in this blessed land. Egypt is the second most mentioned country in the Holy Scripture after Israel, and many prophets of the Old Testament had lived in Egypt, and some of the apostles in the New Testament, such as St. Mark and St. Peter, also came to Egypt. The Holy Family's journey throughout Egypt has been documented and many churches and monasteries exist today on these same grounds, despite years of persecutions against the Copts, occupation by different dynasties and rulers, and many political wars.

St. Mark, the first Patriarch of the Coptic Orthodox Church, preached Christianity in Egypt and was martyred in Alexandria, Egypt on May 8, 58 A.D. St. Mark wrote the first account of the Holy Gospel—although it is placed second in the New Testament books. It is believed that he began writing his account of the Holy Gospel while he was in Italy, but completed it in Egypt. The first ever written Divine Liturgy is also attributed to St. Mark, who was an eyewitness to many of Christ's teachings, exceptional events, and unique experiences of the first apostles in the early Church.

Contributing delegates from the Church of Alexandria were among the most celebrated personalities of the early Church during historic events and ministries: the first three Ecumenical Councils (Nicaea 325 A.D., Constantinople 381 A.D., and Ephesus 431 A.D.), the Theological School of Alexandria, the Didache (Teachings of the Apostles), and Monasticism. Our Church is laden with spiritual wisdom, dogma dating back to the first century of Christianity rooted in the teachings of our Lord Jesus Christ, Holy Tradition delivered from one generation to the next, guidelines for fasting and asceticism, the artistic adornment and veneration of icons, distinctive praises and doxologies, and a myriad of homilies from the most prolific Christian writers of all time. Despite the fact that Christians in Egypt have always been the minority and never did they rule their own country, it is a miracle and a wonder that any Copts exist in Egypt today. All the spiritual writings, teachings, and manuscripts were guarded and remained untainted for preservation against heresies. With limited financial resources, in addition to countless trials and tribulations through the years, it is even a greater wonder how in one half of a century, the Coptic Orthodox Church has flourished with such vigor, conviction, honor, and spiritual beauty throughout the world.

Chapter 2

THE EARLY YEARS OF COPTS IMMIGRATING TO AMERICA

"I sent you to reap that for which you have not labored; others have labored, and you have entered into their labors."

John 4:38

The seemingly glamorous or rather dreary days, depending on the choice of one's lens looking at former Egypt, were soon coming to an end during the 1950's. Egypt had been ruled by several dynasties and monarchies. Gamal Abd-El-Nasser seized the presidency in the early 1950's and gained much support as a patriotic leader. In his efforts, he aimed to expel many non-Egyptians and required that they return to their homelands. Up to that point, Egypt was multicultural, multinational, and multireligious. The Soviet Union was a source of power in Eastern Europe and the United States soon came under the leadership of President John. F. Kennedy in the early 1960's.

During these many years of change and just before the dawn of mass emigration from Egypt began, an unusual phenomenon appeared in Zeitoun, Egypt—a suburb of Heliopolis in the greater Cairo district of Egypt. From 1968-1970, many Egyptians—including Christians, Muslims, and people of other faiths—witnessed the apparition of the Blessed Mother of God, St. Mary. She appeared above the dome of the small church named in her honor. Glistening doves appeared and formed in the shape of a cross preceding her appearances. She blessed the people with the sign of the cross and healed many of all faiths that came to obtain her blessings. The Coptic Orthodox Patriarch of this era was His Holiness Pope Kyrillos VI, who was recently canonized as a saint by the Holy Synod of the Coptic Orthodox Church in June 2013.

While this was happening, the world abroad was embarking on new discoveries in its quest to reach the moon. On July 20, 1969, Neil Armstrong, an American astronaut, was the first man to walk on the moon. In ushered the 1970's and the universe was appearing to be a smaller place, while on the ground was brewing animosity between the United States and Vietnam. Several wars were launched between two of the oldest feuding nations in the world—Egypt and Israel. More homes were having television sets and were able to keep up with the news, as best as possible under the circumstances. The notion of leaving Egypt was growing as many began to assess their future livelihood in their homeland where uncertainty was becoming more certain. Is there a future in Egypt? Will Egypt succumb to Communism? Will there be freedom of religion? Many internal questions were posed but could only be answered by taking the risk of emigration. On the heels of the vast rapid changes in the world, out of Egypt came many sojourners.

The immigration application process was tedious. The countries in the West were primarily interested in professionals. Thus, the first waive of immigrants possessed professional degrees and were able to secure positions in their fields or related fields. This was encouraging, but the few hundred dollars the new immigrants were permitted to take out of Egypt was still insufficient to make ends meet. This posed emotional and economic challenges when arriving in America. Many professionals placed high value on education and had their children enrolled in private schools in Egypt. Due to their financial obligations and limitations, they would have to settle for public schools. There are many exceptional public schools throughout the United States, but I share this information to emphasize the many small and great adaptations that the early immigrants needed to accept. Also, due to their financial restrictions, although many were able to study or work in their professional fields, many also took supplemental jobs to help make up for the deficit in their family budget. Whether in the Untied States or in Egypt, women were just starting to become viable members of the workforce. Many Egyptian women at that time may not have had college degrees from Egypt, and therefore, could not work in professional positions. Thus, some preferred to remain as homemakers, while others settled for positions that could be attained according to their English-speaking skills; and those who could work, they pursued studies to acquire equivalent qualifications of professional degrees that they possessed in Egypt so that they could work in their respective fields in the United States.

The Christian Egyptian community began to form clusters in California and in New Jersey. The first priest commissioned to serve the diaspora in Canada and the United States was Reverend Father Marcos Marcos. Though he resided in Canada, he would frequently travel to locations in the United States to serve the growing population there until priests were either sent to serve them or new priests would be ordained for this ministry. A consortium of different priests was commissioned by His Holiness Pope Kyrillos VI to serve in California, New Jersey, and other states intermittently. Amongst these were the late Rev. Fr. Bishoy Kamel, the late Rev. Ghobrial Abdelsayed, Rev. Fr. Tadros Malaty, and many others who also arrived in the United States and contributed to the establishment of the Christian Orthodox service to the Coptic community in the diaspora. In March 1971, His Holiness Pope Kyrillos VI reposed in the Lord, and His Holiness Pope Shenouda III became his successor, as the 117th Patriarch of the See of St. Mark and the Church of Alexandria. Not long before that, President Gamal Abdel-Nasser also passed away and was succeeded by the second president of Egypt, Anwar El-Sadat.

The Coptic community was delighted to be able to rent churches in the early years until they could afford to buy their own. California and New Jersey were the first states in the United States to purchase churches under their own Coptic title and both were named in honor of St. Mark the Evangelist. Establishing the traditional Sunday school program, as initially designed by the archdeacon, St. Habib

Guirguis—canonized as a saint in June 2013—was the first seed of the spiritual agenda planted in these communities, whether they had their own churches or were renting. Books translating the Divine Liturgies from Arabic, Coptic, and Greek to English were initially a challenge. The first attempt was to use English letters but maintain the original dialect and language. That temporary effort was only until English could be used on its own and had more accurate translations. Other spiritual books were quickly being translated. Bear in mind that these early translations were strictly by typewriters as the computer age had not yet arrived to make computers widely accessible. Thus, minor errors were overlooked, but many revisions soon followed. Many servants, then and now, labored and continue to labor in the formation of the many generations that had emigrated from Egypt and continue to immigrate to the United States. Yet, by the grace of God, we reap the fruits of their labor, which our Good Shepherd, the Lord Jesus Christ, has abundantly increased.

Chapter 3

REFLECTIONS FROM THE FIRST GENERATION OF IMMIGRANTS

"So then neither he who plants is anything, nor he who waters, but God who gives the increase."

1 Corinthians 3:7

St. Athanasius the Apostolic said that St. Anthony the Great was like a bee that trudges, from one hermit to another, seeking nectar for sustenance. Likewise, we can benefit much from the wisdom of our predecessors—clergy and lay men and women that inaugurated the immigration movement into unchartered waters in its infant stages. In this chapter, three of the most distinguished clergy that were early pioneers of immigration to the United States share their experiences, judiciousness, and perception about the comprehensive struggles of the first surge of Coptic immigrants, as well as the clergy's challenges in launching new frontiers while conserving our ancient and sacred dogma, preserving the family unit, and caring for each individual, spiritually, emotionally, and financially. Four lay men and women also share insight and understanding gleaned from their experiences, having embarked on the route of immigration between the late 1960's to the early 1970's.

Reverend Hegumen Father Marcos A. Marcos

A Brief Introduction
I had already studied in the United States for four years before I returned back to Egypt to teach Psychology and Comparative Theology. I did not seek the ordination of the priesthood. When I returned to Egypt, I found out that my father, who was living in Sohag, had a stroke and was in a vegetative state. I wanted to bring my parents to live with me in Cairo where I was living very close to St. Mark's Cathedral.

During that full year, His Holiness Pope Shenouda III (then Bishop Shenouda) was the Dean of the Coptic Theological Seminary. He wanted me to continue teaching in the seminary, but under the condition that I will not become a priest. I told him that I do not want to return to the United States because I have to be with my father. I also promised him that I am not interested in the priesthood. In less than one year, my parents came to live with me in Cairo.

During this time, His Grace Bishop Samuel was in charge of the emigrating Copts. He came to me and said, "I want to see you." I was studying in the United States, and was going from East, to West, to North, and to South, to visit many of the Copts there. At that time, there were no records or census of any form for the Coptic community. I told Bishop Samuel that I think the Copts in the United States are ready to have a priest and he can visit them regularly. When he asked the Copts abroad for a nomination of a candidate for the priesthood, they responded, "We don't know of any other than Wagdy Abd-El-Messih Marcos." Thus, they signed a petition and recommended me.

Caught between the Priesthood and Teaching

When Bishop Samuel saw me, he said, "Now I have the nomination for you for the priesthood." I told him that I promised Bishop Shenouda that I would not be a priest. I also told him about my family situation and that I was also not yet married. He asked, "What do you want me to do; the people want you." I responded, "This is not my calling." The people knew me while I lived and studied on the East Coast in Hartford, Connecticut. During that time, I developed a small pamphlet about different spiritual issues, gave them out to the local community, and mailed them to the Copts in the United States.

Since 1958, I had been mailing this small newsletter to the Copts in the United States. I didn't know many of the people personally, but just by names. We decided to have a retreat starting on Great Friday before the Holy Resurrection Feast. We chose Pennsylvania for our retreat and gathered on Great Friday, Bright Saturday, and Resurrection Sunday. Since there were no churches or priests, we could not celebrate the Divine Liturgy. Therefore, we gathered and just sang some hymns and chanted praises according to these great days. Everyone enjoyed it— even the youth and the children. There were five other servants/counselors beside myself for a total of six serving the adults. Everyone wanted to tell others— and that's how the list grew.

When the numbers grew in the East, we decided to start serving also in other cities as more Copts began moving into other locations. Anyone who had problems would come to any of us for advice. We had good relations with everyone. My studies allowed me ample time to serve more. I became a mediator between the group of servants and the communities. Someone suggested to start an association and have it registered. According to Bishop Samuel's list, there were approximately eighty adults, besides the children and youth, and different services were offered for each age.

Then, I left for Egypt. Because I was the contact person, people knew me. After I returned to Egypt for two years, I was relieved knowing that the new Coptic immigrants were more independent and the association was officially registered. I didn't feel there was any need for me at all there in the United States, and I had not even returned to Connecticut. When Bishop Samuel informed me of the petition that I was nominated for the priesthood by the people in the United States, I responded that I promised Bishop Shenouda that I would remain a layman, and he hired me accordingly. Thus, I reiterated my promise, which I made to Bishop Shenouda, so that I may be excluded from the nomination of the priesthood, again to Bishop Samuel. In addition, I also mentioned that I could not leave my parents and they have already settled down with me. He replied, "I want to see you tomorrow."

I asked, "So, you are not going to give these papers to H.H. Pope Kyrillos?" He didn't seem to give up. The next day, he said he thought of something. He must have prayed. Then, he asked me, if any signs came to me? I said, "None."

Then he said, "I am telling you that if you get any sign, come and tell me." I agreed.

That night, I had a meeting in one of the churches and I came home late. My mother asked me if there was something wrong? I was normal—but just preoccupied. I said, "This world is sometimes like that."

She asked, "What does this all mean?" She realized that I didn't want to reveal what was bothering me. Though my father was home with us, he could not speak because of the stroke. He also could not hear very well, and his vision was also impaired. Sometimes he did not even know me or recognize my name. Finally, I decided to go to sleep, but before I could, my mother asked me to just allow her to sleep comfortably by telling her even a little bit of what was bothering me, so she could sleep. Therefore, I told her what Bishop Samuel said to me, and what I said to him. I told her what I told him, and that was that I could not leave my parents because the commandment says to honor my parents.

From then on, Bishop Samuel would ask me from time to time if there have been any signs. When I would answer, "none," he would just say, "then, keep praying."

Then, one night after I returned from my service meeting in Shubra,[3] my mother awoke me around 1:30 AM. She knocked at the door very loudly and shouted, "Wake up, wake up." I immediately asked about my father, but she said he was fine. Adamantly, she said, "I want to tell you that I am not going to stand against God's service. God will take care of us." I asked her who told her to say that. She said, "Your father." I questioned how he was able to say anything. She replied, "I couldn't sleep, so I was saying your predicament out loud, then I heard your father say, 'Labiba, you are talking about who, Wagdy?'" I asked him if he could hear. He simply replied, 'It is not right. We cannot stand against God's service.'" She said he repeated this twice. My tears ran down my face. I could not say anything for some time.

I did not say anything to Bishop Samuel about what happened that night with my parents, and he did not ask. I thought he forgot. Since I used to take care of his office and translate various papers for him,

---

[3] One of the largest districts of Cairo, Egypt.

I would see him often. About three weeks later, while I was taking an afternoon nap, my mother woke me up and told me that my brother and his wife were at our house and want to say hello. When I went out to meet them, my brother told me to come out to the balcony. He proceeded to tell me that he is my older brother, and of course, I replied, "I know this." Then he began to insist that he is the one who is supposed to take the responsibility of the care of our parents. He added that his wife as well feels the same way. He told me that I still need to get married, and they have prepared a room for our parents with them in Helwan,[4] and with a driver living next door, they can easily transport them as needed. Thus, the plan was suddenly in motion. As of the following Friday, they would come to take our parents and their belongings. I was told that I needed to move on. I really couldn't say either yes or no. I remained quiet; then I revealed to my brother what our father said to our mother that night. Once he heard that, he was even more determined to return the following week to take our parents with him and his wife, which he did.

I prayed for a few days and I couldn't believe it. I was back in Bishop Samuel's office. When I knocked on his door to give him some papers, I noticed a man and his wife were in the office speaking with him.

---

[4] Southern suburb of Cairo, Egypt.

When I realized that the man was weeping, I was too embarrassed to enter; so I excused myself. Bishop Samuel then insisted that I enter. Out of compassion for this crying man, I kept trying to excuse myself from entering the room. Bishop Samuel proceeded to introduce us to each other. This man and his wife were both physicians and faculty professors—well known and respected in the community.

Bishop Samuel then turned to the crying man and told him, "This is the man I was telling you about." Then, he finally began to explain this couple's circumstances. They had a son who was living in Los Angeles, California. Not having many young single Coptic women in the United States at that time, he married an American woman. Unfortunately, the marriage was in trouble. They had a child together, but his wife was depriving him of seeing their child. Bishop Samuel then told me that he has a plane ticket for me to Los Angeles and asked me to please go and resolve this issue. He turned to the man and explained to him that they were thinking to send this person (me) to be ordained a priest and to serve the Copts in the United States. Confidently, His Grace turned to me and said, "Assure them, Wagdy."

But, I responded, "I can't Your Grace."

He just answered, "Okay, we will talk tomorrow."

So far, I have shared three out of five signs. The fourth sign was a rather long case that does not need any detail. Needless to say, it was a case concerning a girl who emigrated to America and then converted to another religion. The fifth sign was attached to the initial promise, which I made to Bishop Shenouda and I was determined to keep it by teaching courses at the Seminary and not accepting the candidacy of the priesthood. Thus far, I had kept my promise, and it was my second year of teaching.

A Heated Discussion among Four Bishops and a Priest
Bishop Samuel spoke to His Eminence Bishop Domadius of Giza (elevated to His Eminence Metropolitan Domadius on June 2, 1985). They made a plan that four bishops and a priest (Hegomen Father Salib Sorial) would pray the Divine Liturgies at a very near date that was set. I did not know at the time, but this group of bishops also included His Grace Bishop Athanasius of Beni Suef (elevated to His Eminence Metropolitan Athanasius on June 18, 1978), and surprisingly, also His Grace Bishop Shenouda, the Dean of the Theological Seminary where I taught, and who would become our beloved 117th Patriarch on November 14, 1971.

Five Liturgies were prayed, and when the bishops reconvened and finished their lunch, they started having what you may call a "social hour." So, one of the bishops asked Bishop Samuel, who was recently back from a year of study in America and was also visiting the Copts across the land, the question, "Your Grace, why don't you tell us about the status of the Copts who settled in America; what are their numbers? Do they have churches there? Are they being cared for spiritually?"

Bishop Samuel answered saying: "The numbers have increased and I think that they are ready now to have a priest to cater for their spiritual needs."

At that point, Bishop Shenouda strongly entered into the discussion and said: "Listen now, we are not going to make the same mistake we did with Ethiopia." Bishop Shenouda was referring to Bishop Makarios who was sent to Ethiopia as a Coptic bishop. Unfortunately, he did not speak the language (Amharic), nor did he know their customs, the habits, the rituals, etc. Therefore, the bishop could not stay in Ethiopia except for two months per year. This caused many divisions in the church at that time. Bishop Shenouda continued, "If we are going to send someone to America, he has to be someone who lived there, speaks the language, is familiar with the customs, etc. If we are going to send a priest there, he has to acquire those qualities."

Here, Bishop Athanasius said, "Your Grace, whom do you recommend?"

Bishop Shenouda responded, "If you want to take Wagdy [my unworthy self], take him if he agrees. It is alright with me."

Then, Bishop Samuel asked Bishop Shenouda, "Please, you speak to Wagdy, he will listen to you," which he did the following day. A day or two later, I met Bishop Samuel and he told me that he will give me a copy of the list of Copts who nominated my undeserving self for the priesthood. I told His Grace that I had one condition condition: that I will not leave my teaching role until the end of the academic year, and he agreed. During that year, I got engaged and soon after, Tasoni[5] Suzy and I were married.

Peaceful Ending

Two weeks later, on August 9, 1964, His Holiness the Saint Pope Kyrillos VI delegated Bishop Athanasius of Beni Suef to perform the Priest's Ordination prayers and the ritual of the laying of the hands at St. Mark's Cathedral of Azbakiya. His Grace Bishop Athanasius declared loudly: "We ordain you Marcos, priest for God's altar of the Coptic Orthodox Church of North

---

[5] "Tasoni" is a Coptic word meaning "my sister." It is a term of endearment and title commonly used to address the wife of a priest.

America..."⁶ During that time my tears would not cease from falling.

New priests always spend the first forty days of their priesthood in the monastery; however, Pope Kyrillos told me to stay with him during these forty days, so I received this immense blessing from his beloved hands. Since then, my service took me to many places and rarely was I to return home. Though I didn't ask for it or seek it, it was God's plan for me.

Emigration was not an easy requisite. I was supposed to go to Rome for Vatican II in 1964, after I finished the courses that I was teaching. At that time, I was taking all the items for the liturgical services, the vestments, altar settings, utensils, and other important items. I needed an exit visa, which had some requirements—listing the countries to where I would be traveling. I wrote three down: Italy, Canada, and the United States. When they saw these, they refused, saying, "absolutely not." According to President Gamal Abd-El-Nasser, no one was allowed to travel to America or Canada, at least not with such ease.

I explained that I was traveling to Italy as a representative of the Coptic Orthodox Church. Furthermore, I explained that our church is the only church that says that the biblical verse, "His blood be

---

⁶ The name "Marcos" was chosen by H.H. Pope Kyrillos and the wording of the ordination was prepared by both His Holiness the Pope and Bishop Athanasius.

on us and on our children," (Matthew 27:25) is literal. I emphasized this statement to prove my loyalty, first of all to the Holy Scripture, and also to Egypt, since at that time, the Egyptian Copts had the wrong reputation of being sympathetic to Israel.

The man in charge said to go to Italy and return, and then try again for America and Canada. I tried to convince him, but he said maybe in two-three years time. I told him again that I am serving my country because my mission in Italy is to explain this scriptural verse to them, but then, I would not return. We argued at length—each one trying to prove his point. The convention was starting in one week. I asked him to give me the visa so I could leave, or otherwise, I will stay there in Cairo. I told him that he would be held responsible if I do not attend. I represent my Church. After I made my case, I was finally able to leave by Sunday morning to the Vatican. I stayed two and a half months in Rome.

The position of the clergy that was predominantly from the West was to proclaim that the Jewish people could not be held accountable for their ancestors' proclamation. I wrote three pages and made two hundred copies and put them in the big center in the Vatican. When my greeter realized what happened, he asked me, "What have you done? You cannot enter anyone's quarters, especially these high scholars of the Vatican; you just cannot. These are the rules and they are written. The Synod comprising of six hundred members here will accuse you. Just apologize and say you did not know." So I took the responsibility of my actions and told them the truth—that the person that was supposed to meet me could not come, so I did not know. I am responsible for everything written here. I asked them to forgive me. They looked at each other and then assured me everything was all right.

One of these VIPs translated my documents consisting of the three pages and gave them to a journalist. The journalist highlighted, "The representative of the Coptic Orthodox Church, as usual, has issues..." By 6:00 in the evening, the Ambassador of Egypt to the Vatican called me to tell me that I did what no one else could do. He wanted to come to me, but I told him to give me his address and I would go to him. I did not want anyone to think that the embassy had anything to do with my comments. We had a nice dinner and then he gave me a large envelope and told me that its contents are for me to use for site seeing. I told him frankly that I do not accept any money. This is a service to my church before my country. He kept insisting to offer me something, but I refused.

We talked and I explained that my wife was to come and join me. So the hotel moved my luggage from my hotel, which was for the singles to the one for couples. In the second hotel's dining room, each table was arranged to seat couples. My table was the only one that had only three people sharing a meal for four. Indeed it was embarrassing. I was always asked the same questions, "Where is your wife?" My answer was, "She is awaiting her exit visa."

I asked the Ambassador, "Do you not think that this gives a bad image of Egypt?"

The Ambassador asked me, "Would you allow me to interfere?"

I said, "Please do." He took Suzy's information and assured me that she will come in less than a week. Indeed, after four days, I was waiting for her at Rome's Airport. She stayed with me for about one month. Then, we flew to North America, stopping to meet the Copts and attending Divine Liturgies—first in Canada (Montreal, then Ottawa, then to Toronto), then New York City in the United States, and then back to Toronto. New York was the place of the original headquarters that was taking care of our expenses, but my residence was in Toronto.

There were many difficult experiences in the first few early years. There was a group that was against the church and would have their own meetings. They wanted to establish a social Christian club for the Copts in Toronto. None of them asked about the priest, or the church, and wanted to drive the priest away. So I thought, we will work with the few that we have. Their children, of course, did not have any contact with the church either. We were still renting at this time—just for dollars. All the lands and rentals, and even when we requested more space, were just for a single dollar. We only paid $1.00!

Prior to my ordination, I was involved in creating the Coptic association and providing spiritual and practical advice. When I returned two years later as a priest, the five other servants that used to serve with me had already dispersed. Unfortunately, the association had transformed the bylaws and added elements according to their own desires. With new members and a new agenda, it became a new board. When I returned in 1964, it was not a spiritual association, but rather a social organization. I began to work with them under their rules. The board was the supporter of the church. I had to abide. It was ironic that my former professor of psychology in the theological seminary was the head of the board. They greeted me well.

Thus, my mission as a priest began. I wanted to take a trip around the United States and Canada. However, the board declared that there were now new rules. I could attend their meetings, but I am employed by the association and receive a salary. It hurt, but I let it go. They had to approve my trip and it was their decision which cities and which states I could visit. I did not say anything so I could maintain unity of thought amongst us. They asked me to bring them all my expenses. Eventually, I left for my journey and returned about two months later. I was concerned about what to say to people that live in places that I was not allowed to visit. I deeply regretted not being able to address their needs. I was only allowed to go to the big cities. Many people called and said they needed to be served, they needed a baptism for a child, they had problems, and for many other reasons they specified, but I could not go to them.

When I returned, I informed the treasurer that more visitations were needed. Unyielding, he affirmed that I must abide by what was said by the board. I thought to myself that even though money was scarce, maybe later when these people receive help, are spiritually served, and have an opportunity to know the Church more, they would contribute generously and help support it. I contacted the head of the board, but he reiterated the same slogan as the treasurer and secretary, which is that I must abide by their rules. So I agreed because the head of the board was my seminary professor and I respected him.

I thought to myself, it is truly better to obey God than man.[7] I told the people, we would have to postpone some plans. When I returned to Toronto, I shared my thoughts and experiences with the small congregation. They said they must help. However, their help was going to the headquarters in New York. There were genuine concerns. If someone passes away and lives in a far state, must I not go and pray over the deceased? What if someone is very ill, this person's blood will be required from the father—the priest? Correct. I told them I got their point. They said they would help. Five or six of them got the airline tickets and I informed the treasurer that my travels were no longer the board's concerns. He replied that it is of their concern. I told him that I am responsible to God, and it is better to obey God than man. My professor called me and questioned why. I had to admit to him that my conscience would not allow me to just leave anyone in need like this; otherwise, I would return to Egypt. I offered to return their money and their tickets, but asked for some time to inform my congregation. He replied that the board would continue to support me for the next six months. So I left on my trip, and then finally to New York, and then to Toronto.

---

[7] Acts 5:29.

Of course, there were a lot of protests against my decision. My professor understood my perspective. We agreed that I will do some things their way; and the things they don't approve, I will do on my own. Next, another gentleman, Mr. Habashi,[8] invited us to his home to have a meeting. I suggested that we go separate ways. Mr. Habashi told me that I am a priest and we are registered as an organization. I told him that I could not serve under these kinds of circumstances and kill my conscience. Many protests and heated arguments followed. I stayed quiet and was very sad. I had nothing—no bishop, no support, no money, nothing. This was one of the hardest times. Mr. Habashi sent me $1000 for a donation and a plane ticket—one-way to Egypt, and said, "We are not ready for a priest." I returned it. The Church is under the authority of none, but God.

I returned to Toronto and took some time for a retreat at an Anglican monastery with Fr. Palmer, an Anglican priest. I prayed and asked God to be with me. I told our treasurer that I am no longer part of that organization, and that I don't want the name of the church under this association name at all anymore. Furthermore, I told him that as of the following months, to not send me anything. My professor was

---

[8] Mr. Saba Pasha Habashi. Pasha is a word of Turkish origin. Mr. Habashi was a high-ranking government official in the government of King Farouk.

upset. The people in Toronto vowed to support our church. We wrote the bylaws and separated. My trips would sometimes take seven weeks instead of five weeks. After one to two years, we were reconciled with Bishop Samuel's guidance, and most of them began to attend church regularly with us. I decided to share this experience with the readers now so that others would learn from this experience and not repeat the same mistakes.

The best experience was very educational. In Toronto, three devoted families soon became seventeen families. God's work with us exceeded everyone's expectations. Some people may have wanted to drive the priests away; while the others were very devoted and spiritually thirsty. God really blessed us a lot. We did not have money or churches—really nothing at all. I got to know some other priests from other local churches of different denominations. One elderly priest from the Anglican Church—Fr. Palmer—came to me one day and asked where we were all praying now. There was thoughtful interest in our church by our neighbors. I replied to his question by saying the truth—really anywhere. He said he wants to visit me at home, so I welcomed him. He came and brought another priest with him. To my surprise, they said they want to have the blessing of the ancient Liturgy that we pray. Apparently, he knew about the Coptic Orthodox Church and used to attend a theological school in Toronto.

I learned many things from him. He visited many Coptic Churches. He brought my attention to a fascinating detail, which we pray, in every Liturgy. He asked me why it is that when we make our supplications or petitions in prayer during the Liturgy, all other churches say, "Amen," except the Coptic Church? I searched and searched and finally discovered by the help of Fr. Palmer, that it is because we consider ourselves unworthy to ask God for this blessing. We say we do not deserve it, so we ask for His mercy; not according our deeds, but according to His mercy,[9] that it is why we say, "Lord have mercy." I had not even asked, but God was teaching me many things.

I learned a lot from Fr. Palmer. When he did not see me for a long time because I was traveling often, he would ask about me. One day, he confronted me with kindness and said, "You did not tell me that another Coptic priest came to America." He was very interested in the Church and knew that Reverend Fr. Mikhail arrived and was serving in Cleveland, Ohio. Fr. Palmer knew this because of the little newsletter I used to send. I apologized, but asked him why he would want to know about him? He replied, "I have a list of all the names of the Coptic priests in North

---

[9] Divine Liturgy.

America. But because I did not know about him, I have not prayed for him for the last two months because I did not know he was here. I wish that I was young like you so I could go with you and tell your people that your Church is full of treasures." From 1964-1977, many churches of other denominations offered their church buildings to us for free to use for prayer and services. In April 1977, His Holiness Pope Shenouda III of the thrice blessed memory on his first visit to Canada laid the cornerstone for the first Coptic Orthodox Church built in North America. Miraculously, we purchased 1.1 acre for $1.00 to build the church. We received the keys to the church on April 23, 1978. It took us only one year to build the church.

I was one of the board members and we were looking for land, but couldn't find anything reasonable. One of the other board members said that if we were Protestants, we could get something for half the cost. I said, "God will provide."

He said, "We may have something here for half the cost," and added, "God be with you."

There was a Protestant man that does not give any preferences to anyone other than Protestants. So one day, I approached him and told him I had heard about him. I told him I am coming to him to ask about building the first Coptic Orthodox Church in North

America. He listened briefly, and then referred me to his son, an attorney, so I went to him next. The son referred me back to his father. So I returned to the father. The father then informed me that he is going to the hospital on the following day; but after he came out of the hospital, he would not return my calls. He was very elderly.

I waited for six months, then I called the son again, who referred me back to his father again. This continued for two years. I prayed and decided to call the elderly father again. I asked him if he had forgotten about me. He asked if we (the Coptic community) have been there all this time? He also asked me about the name of the church and why we want the land. Again, I explained. Then, he instructed me to call his son. I told him that I did already—many times. He asked from where is my accent, and what exactly our church is? I told him again that it is an Orthodox Church. He then said to talk to his son—but not today, tomorrow. He told me then to just listen and call him before 8:30 AM at his home number. He asked, "Don't you know it?" So I called, and he did remember, but this time, he told me to go see him in his office, on Thursday. I went with the board secretary and took a book for him by Dr. Aziz Sorial Attia entitled, "The History of Eastern Christianity."

He thanked me and asked what it was we wanted? I explained that we want to build a church according to the design and custom of the Coptic Orthodox heritage. He asked about the size of the land that we were seeking. My reply was about one to two acres. He wanted to know exactly where we were seeking. I said, "Anywhere." I explained that many people would like to live near the church, so anywhere would be fine.

Again, he asked, "If you have a choice, then where?"

Again, I said, "anywhere."

He asked again, where would we choose the area to be? I kept confirming that any area would be fine for us. He insisted that we tell him exactly where we want to build our church, saying, "I want to know what your needs are." Finally, I told him about a particular nice area. He asked if I was sure—and as if to be certain of the location, he asked if I meant in this particular area near certain crossroad streets. This area was going to be perfect for us. He agreed.

So finally, I asked the difficult question, "How much will it cost?" He smiled and wrote $1.00 with a light pencil on the map that had city streets on it. I thought he was joking, but he assured me he was not kidding. The secretary put on his glasses and saw the same thing. I tried to clarify my question, so I said, "I mean the money that you will take."

He responded, "If you have $1.00, the land is yours."

I asked, "Why are you giving it to me for $1.00." He revealed that after I spoke with his father, the elderly man went to him and told him that if this land was suitable, then to give it to us for $1.00. Apparently, this was the land upon which they had agreed before I had even chosen it for our church.

When I was speaking with Bill McLintock, the landowner, it was understood that the $1.00 was just a formality to actually pay some money so that it can be registered as a purchase. I announced the great news to the people about the purchase of the land and everyone wanted to see it. Regardless of the rain, we headed over to the land and stood in the rain with newspapers on our heads—and we were all praying. There I was as a priest—praying and sprinkling water on this land that was being showered upon by God. We finished our prayers and returned to our homes. What we needed to do now was build. Everyone started to donate from their own savings, more than just their tithing. These many overwhelming blessings far exceeded everyone's imaginations. I still continued to pray for the former board, and eventually, they became members of our congregation. His Grace Bishop Antonios of Sohag consecrated the land, and ultimately, the Thrice Blessed Pope Shenouda III visited us and blessed us. In 2014, His Holiness Pope Tawadros II consecrated the new St. Mark Cathedral, which is just minutes away from our historic church and humble beginnings. It was indeed a great honor and a cherished blessing to have His Holiness amongst us, and for my abject self, that His Holiness personally attended the jubilee anniversary of my priesthood ordination. God has been working with us so wonderfully throughout the years. We always felt that God's hand was filled with more than what we asked and even thought. Glory be to His name.

Reverend Hegumen Father Tadros Y. Malaty

I came to the United States in 1970. At that time, Fr. Pishoy Kamel had come before me in 1969 and stayed for ten months. He was responsible for more than one half of the United States. I replaced him and served in America for two years and three months because he had to return to Egypt. Fr. Pishoy and I were always happy to do as the Pope wishes. Pope Kyrillos VI did not force Fr. Pishoy Kamel to go to the United States, but rather told him it is all right if he did not want to go. Fr. Pishoy responded that he wants to go so if anyone asks him about immigration, he will have the experience and can share it and offer advice.

At that time, the church had no experience on immigration. Nobody knew the circumstances of new immigrants. I was initially commissioned to serve in California. The priest in California was also responsible for many other locations, including: Los Angeles, San Francisco, Portland, Seattle, Dallas, Houston, Minneapolis, and Denver. Every week, I would usually go on Friday and return on Saturday, although sometimes I would stay at the location two nights. In Houston, there were about twenty-five to thirty families; five families in Dallas; five hundred families in Los Angeles; thirty in San Francisco; and a few in Denver. We would pray two Divine Liturgies, have Bible studies, and I would take their confessions.

For me, nothing is difficult in my life. When I am asked what year was I ordained, my response is, "Every morning, I am ordained a priest." If we trust in the years and times, these will collapse. Every day is the most joyful day. I feel it was a divine plan for my edification, for the glory of God, and for the glory of the Church. As a priest, nothing is ever difficult. The source of my happiness is God, as it was also for Fr. Pishoy Kamel—to serve God and to do as the Pope wishes. Fr. Pishoy and I did not encourage immigration at first, but when we came, we enjoyed the service here. I have a passion for writing and studying. At that time in Egypt, Gamal Abd-El-Nasser was strongly against the United States and did not allow anyone to bring anything from there. However, it was a good time for me to study and to bring books about the fathers to Egypt without any problems.

In the first few years in Los Angeles, California, there was a new movement. Young people, married and single, saw the Church as their mother. I remember just a few cases of family problems. It was a new atmosphere. The church doors were always open and the United States was much safer. My wife and I did not have to lock the doors of our home or the church. Many of the young people were servants. It was a community of love. My role was to teach and work on behalf of the Church. It was not just fun.

The first few years were a totally different experience. When I first arrived in the United States, the main problem for the immigrants was that they could not return back to Egypt. The regime of the government at that time would not accept any of them to return because they were perceived as disloyal to Egypt. Thus, the new immigrants feared they would never see their parents until they died. They stressed about how they can live in the United States, but remain deprived from their families, their churches, and the monasteries in Egypt. This policy regarding the perception of disloyalty of immigrants changed after the presidency of Anwar El-Sadat.

The first generation of Coptic immigrants to the United States were well educated and could find work or continue with their advanced academic or research studies. Their problems were simple and their main issue was that they lost their connection with Egypt because of the Egyptian policy regarding emigrants and loyalty. The second group came under pressure. This group commonly did not come directly from Egypt. Nonetheless, the two groups were loving and accepting towards each other. The problems were less. Nowadays, we are in need to go to every house and to take care of every house personally.

Many new immigrants today are from villages, Upper and Lower Egypt, and some can't read English or even Arabic. Nowadays, the immigrants' problems are more difficult. Children speak English, but their parents cannot. Thus, the leaders of these families become the children. The parents and their children are disconnected from each other. It is not a matter of money, but who will lead and direct the family? The Church has to find solutions for the family, especially when there is no contact between parents and the children. Some churches thought to teach the children Arabic by providing lessons in the Arabic language. Speaking Arabic was really not the problem, but rather the parents needed to learn to speak English so that they may communicate with their children and lead their families. Issues facing other newcomers today are when their former high socioeconomic statuses contrasts drastically with their new reality in the United States. Many have to start at just any level. They lose their identity and some experience depression because of this loss of identity.

When immigration began, the priests that came were able to communicate in either language, Arabic or English. Now, some priests come because their children are here. In other Orthodox Churches, and also in the the Catholic Church, they mandate seminars to teach the priests how to deal with people about practical matters and to progress and help the new generation. I think we are in need, not just of seminars or lectures, but to discuss and apply practical measures. Many of the priests are looking for buildings and focusing on social problems, which are also important, but sometimes, we ignore salvation. How can we educate our children to witness to the Lord Jesus Christ? We were oppressed in Egypt, but now, it is different. It is not just about learning history, but how to live full of love with a fiery heart, and how to attract every person to our Lord Jesus Christ. Priests need to know how to give a chance to every single person, from the child to the old man, to be an active member, not just in a material way, or as a deacon, or making the eulogia (corban).[10] The Church offers supplications in every Divine Liturgy, sermons, and in personal prayers that God may reveal Himself to all mankind—especially in the United States, regardless if they are Egyptian or from any other ethnicity or origin.

I believe the problem here with immigrants is the person feels alone. The bishop, priest, and servants, are sometimes impersonal. The new immigrant feels there is no personal touch—just hymns and sermons. It is more important to know how the person feels, and to convey the essential message that God the Father is in every home, or otherwise, no one can feel the motherhood of the Church. There is much lacking on this point. Many complaints from young people are that they do not feel that the leaders are in fact the representatives of the Holy Trinity.

The churches here are taking care of all the needs of the newcomers according to their circumstances. People cannot always work in any kind of job or as they did in Egypt. They are also in need, not only in solving their problems, but to be in touch with love. They feel they are alone, far from their families, and isolated from their communities. Without mentioning any particular cities, I asked the priest at this one church how many families are in his congregation. He

---

[10] Holy Bread (cf. Mark 7:11).

said about three hundred. Then I asked him, when he was ordained about three years prior, how many times he visited all of them. How many daily visits does he do? He responded one-two visits daily. I told him that when I was in Los Angeles, I used to visit between five-seven families daily—at least.

I used to serve in Melbourne, Australia for three years and a half. My service included preaching, teaching Patrology, Sunday school, and equipping the servants of more than five hundred families. I would also contact them by phone. I remember that once I visited twenty families in one day. I would find out when they work and made my visitation schedule accordingly. I visited more than four hundred families in three months. The problem is when that priest, which I mentioned, was ordained, nobody told him what to do and what his responsibilities are regarding visitations. We are in need for new priests to have experience on how to seriously accomplish visitations.

I want to admit something very important. We have a chance today—maybe not tomorrow. Some newcomers need translations. It is a good opportunity to translate spiritual literature from Arabic to English for the new generations to help them feel they have a special purpose. How many Copts in the United States are writers? We are in need. I made a DVD consisting of over two hundred books and I asked those who read it, not just to edit it, but to also rewrite what I wrote.

I feel that today many of our sermons and books are very literal. Rarely do we find books by fiery hearts to see the heavenly light. I have heard people say they go to the Orthodox Church just to receive Holy Communion, but they actually prefer to go to other churches to hear the sermons. This is very dangerous. We have to write books concerning the Orthodox dictionary—not just the words, but real terms for living a Christian life written in a very spiritual and practical way. When we ask people in church about their experiences, they remember their faults and sins; they confess and they take communion; but the talk is generally focused on the negatives. We need to stress the positives. The confessor needs to return to God the Father, to return to the Lord Jesus Christ, and to return to the Holy Spirit. I feel these people are depressed because of their sins. What about the grace of God and loving Christ and the Holy Trinity? We are in need to revisit the fathers' discourses regarding returning to God. God is the forgiver of sins and God grants special glory for you and me in heaven. It is about all of our definitions. Church terms must be written in a Patristic way.

Immigrants' struggles differ from one person to another. It is the work of the Church to bring their members to a better understanding. They have to struggle not just for grades in academics or at work, but with sincerity in love. You are called to be with the Lord and all the heavenly hosts are waiting to see you and to welcome you. Your happiness is not from the outside but from the inner man. The Holy Spirit is working in you. Live this way and you will find happiness.

I hope in our writings, conferences, worship, and personal and communal lives that the goal is very clear as to why I am serving the Holy Trinity. This is the mission of the Church—to reveal the fatherhood of the Father, the redeeming work and love of the Lord Jesus Christ, and the sanctification and renewal of our inner man by the Holy Spirit. This must be very clear in every sermon or it is a failure in fulfilling our mission.

I want also to add a remark. Since the time we started in 1968, none of us have been separated from each other. I remember many persons in the Greek Church who visited me had no idea what has been published. They saw a variety of different books and insisted I send them some. So, I sent ten-twenty books free—nothing for sale. I also sent to our priests, but when I visited this one priest, I was surprised to find the parcel I sent had not been opened for six months. We are becoming more isolated from each other. Its time to return to the basic principles of love through spiritual and practical Orthodox Christianity as taught to us by the Fathers of the Church—before it is too late.

Reverend Hegumen Father Bishoy Gobreial
(1928–2014)

In Memoriam: Reverend Hegumen Father Bishoy Gobreial reposed in the Lord on Sunday September 14, 2014 before this book was printed. With a generous heart, he shared his sincere reflections, wisdom, and kindness with everyone. May the Lord repose the precious soul of His faithful servant in the Paradise of Joy.

I moved from Egypt to America because the education in Egypt was very bad. It was too competitive and there was too much discrimination. There was no future for young people, and no ways for them to find good jobs. I was looking to give my children a better future. When I decided that was what I wanted to do, I considered immigrating to the United States.

Emigrating was a very easy decision because I felt strongly that in the future, there would not be good opportunities in Egypt for my children. That is why I decided to immigrate to the United States, Canada, or Australia. I started first with the United States of America. If they refused me, then I would have applied to Canada, and if they had refused me, I would have tried Australia. The decision was very easy. It was not hard for me to leave my family because every few years we would go back to see them.

Being able to immigrate was hard, but we were encouraged by an encounter we had with Pope Kyrillos VI. We went to see His Holiness and my wife asked him to help us find a new apartment, a bigger one, because our children were outgrowing it and needed a larger place to live. When she said that to him, he said, "Why do you want an apartment? You are going to emigrate. You don't need it." That's why I had a strong will to emigrate. After that, I put the application for emigration on the altar of St. Mary of Zeitoun. After the visit with Pope Kyrillos, we received the approval of the application—about five or six months later. The government was going to cancel the applications of all the people who were going to emigrate because the president at the time said that we were a growing country and needed the youth to help the country to develop. Therefore, no one else would be allowed to emigrate. The people complained in the newspapers and everywhere. After four months, he said that if anyone got their resignations before a certain day, then they could emigrate. I got my resignation on the last day possible. And by that, the word of Pope Kyrillos VI was fulfilled.

After emigrating to California, I became acquainted with the Rev. Fr. Luke Sidarous (the current priest of the Abu Sefein Church in Torrance, CA, who formerly served at the Church of St. Mark in Los Angeles, where I was at the time). During the prayers of the Kiahk month on one Saturday night, he asked to talk to me; so I went with him to his office and he said to me, "We think and we've decided (the entire congregation) that we want you to be the priest of this church because I have to go to Egypt and I want you to replace me." I told him, "I cannot be a priest at all; you have this man, this man, this man…" I mentioned many names. I never ever thought to be a priest even for one moment, not a single moment. Fr. Luke said, "If it is from God, it will go on. If it is against God, it will stop." That night, I went into the sanctuary and prayed with tears asking God what I should do because I never thought that one day I would be a priest, at all—never for a moment.

Priests must first of all be very humble and not pay attention to the opinions of people but of the opinion of God because God examines the hearts of everyone. They should serve humbly and treat all of the people in the same manner. By serving this way, they will be successful in their service. I was going to work in the hospital in the San Fernando Valley and I attended an exam and passed. They said to me that

Chapter Three: Reflections from the First Generation of Immigrants

after a few days I would receive a letter asking when I would like to start my job. After three days, there was a severe earthquake and the hospital was damaged, and I did not get the position; but I thank God that the earthquake did not happen during the exam.

When His Holiness Pope Shenouda III was traveling during his first visit to London, he talked to Fr. Luke and asked to see the new priest candidate before he goes to Egypt (for the traditional 40-day training held in the monastery immediately following a priest's ordination). He told Fr. Luke to tell me to go to London. I prayed and said, "My Lord, I will go to London. If you accept for me to be a priest, I will continue my journey to Egypt. If you do not, I will return to Los Angeles." I talked to the Pope and he asked who my father confessor was and inquired about how I serve within the church. He then said that he was going to Egypt on February 9th and that he wanted me to accompany him there. He then said that we will go to the monastery together and that he was going to ordain me over there.

When I arrived in Egypt, I met him at his car, and by chance, I also met Rev. Fr. Tadros Yacoub Malaty and his wife Tasoni Mary. He asked me what happened? I told him everything. Then he went to Pope Shenouda and said, "Fr. Pishoy Kamel wants to attend the ordination of the new priest." He asked if we could have the ordination at St. George in Sporting, Alexandria instead of at the monastery. Pope Shenouda replied, "Anything that Fr. Pishoy Kamel asks, I will do."

His Holiness told me, "Stay the week with your family in Egypt and next Saturday, we will go to St. George and we will sleep at the church, and then on Sunday February 18th, you will be ordained."

I slept at the church with Fr. Tadros on the 17th and I was ordained as the priest for the St. Mark Coptic Orthodox Church in Los Angeles, California on February 18, 1979. From there, I went to the St. Pishoy monastery to learn how to pray the Divine Liturgy, and was assigned to one of the monks who helped me (Fr. Tadros St. Pishoy). Three weeks later, I met His Grace Bishop Pachomius (elevated to His Eminence Metropolitan Pachomius on September 2, 1990). He said to me, "When you complete the forty days at St. Pishoy monastery, I want you to come to where I pray and preach instead of me among the people."

I told him, "I am still new; how can I pray and preach to the people instead of you? That is very hard." He told me that I could do it; then he put it in his notes. I went there, attended the Bible study, and I preached. It was my first time preaching. I remember the topic was water in the Holy Bible. I remember that it went well. Some people took notes. Some of the priests came up to me and told me I did well, and as a new priest, it was very good. Bishop Pachomius introduced me to the people and they thanked me. After that, I came to my church in Los Angeles, CA.

Those who were immigrants in my time weren't too many. They would go to church regularly, but now some people come without any knowledge of the English language. Some do not even know how to write or read Arabic. That's why they face many difficulties. If someone wants to emigrate, they should study the language of the country to which they are going. It is very hard to emmigrate because there are not enough jobs. It is hard to find employment. Many American graduates cannot even find work and spend many years unemployed.

The best experience I have had was being able to live near to the church. This was a blessing. We used to go to church every week and my kids were ordained as deacons[11] in the church. They started to study the hymns of the church and that made me so happy. It allowed us to be together and share in a relationship with God. I would advise newcomers to submit themselves in the hands of the Lord. The Lord is the Almighty God. All the people are in is

---

[11] By this he means one of the "minor orders" (usually chanter, or reader). In the Coptic Church, the term "deacon" is broadly applied to refer to all the minor orders as well as an actual deacon.

hands. He is going to give everyone as they need. That is why I advise them to be very close to God and to put all of their problems in His hands. He will solve all of their problems at the time that He wants. Since the Lord accepted that people come here, that means that there is something here for them. The Lord will give them what they need according to His time and not according to their time. They have to come to church every week. The church is ready to help everyone according to their experience, and by this they can find a way to live until the Lord gives them new employment opportunities in order to be able to support their families. It is very important to go to church and talk to people, as many are eager to help.

Mr. Peter I

The aftermath of World War II stirred tremendously the "winds of change" in the world, especially in developing countries, like Egypt, which had many challenges. In this turmoil, change affected everything: countries, kingdoms, communities, groups, and individuals—you name it.

As one of the individuals living in this chaotic time, I had an opportunity to move to a land I envisioned had a better standard of living. I firmly believed this opportunity was a dream come true. I felt I had to take this chance, come what may. Once in the United States of America, one of the challenges I had to face was how to start a new life and living in an estranged country about which I knew not enough, especially with the meager maximum amount of $500.00, with which we were allowed to emigrate. So be it. I will take the chance with my wife and two small children in a land of immense competition where a person had to have some skill to succeed.

Other pertinent problems which immigrants experienced were a lack of means and knowledge to make ends meet. How and where to start had to be learned by trial and error. Some immigrants were lucky, some were quick learners, and some may have lagged behind. The majority, however, and I was one of them, were willing to "toil and trouble," with patience, perseverance, and faith in God. And this is how I made it. The ongoing challenges to many of us remain as we try to to deal with the many facets that exist in American culture, on the one hand, and the deep-rooted legacies of the Copts, on the other.

Dr. Nevine G.

In 1967, I arrived in the United States with my parents and younger brother. Even at the young age of seven years old, I could comprehend the enormity of this life-changing event. All of the sudden, I no longer had my beloved Teta Mimi and my favorite Aunt Suzy around me. Everyone spoke a language I could not understand. I went from a sprawling old apartment with several family members to love and with whom I interacted frequently, to a small, barren, cold studio apartment in the heart of chilly Chicago. No longer was I the center of loving family attention. I was now required to be responsible for the care of my younger, and may I say, extremely active two-year-old brother, as my parents were preoccupied with finding employment.

Needless to say, I am very sympathetic to the plight of those young people that find themselves in a new world—fish out of water. As an adult, the decision is made to make the epic move, but as a child, you have no such choice, and so accepting the consequences is quite difficult. There is, however, a huge silver lining to these circumstances. Growing up in this unique situation has made me strong, resilient, perseverant, and given me a deep reliance on God. It is imperative that newcomers "stick like glue" to our beloved Coptic Church. It will prove to be the lighthouse that will guide everyone through many storms.

It is difficult to grow up in a "culture within a culture," and so my saving grace was the group of girls from our church in Chicago with whom I routinely spent time. We attended Sunday school together, hymns classes, Coptic classes, had sleep overs, and went on numerous outings. They were the ones that made me feel that I am not so "different" after all. We had similar rules at home, traditions, restrictions, and our own little language. I grew to appreciate the unique and wonderful aspects of our Egyptian culture and Coptic heritage, but also I grew to appreciate the tremendous aspects of the American culture that allowed me to eventually excel in my education, career, and personal life.

Currently, at 54 years old, I have concentrated my efforts to serving the young people of our church, high school Sunday school, and the college group. As much as I am able, I try to provide as much time for camaraderie and fellowship as is possible so as to give them precious time together—based on my own experience. It is important that we are compassionate with those young newcomers that must overcome the difficulties of this life-changing move. It is not enough to provide financial help—that is of course needed—but also an ear to listen, open arms, and a compassionate heart. Give them your cell number so that they may call you at any time, even just to have you translate to a store clerk! It is important to have the overall feeling that we have been there and we are all in this together! With the grace of God, we will all prevail.

Mr. Nader A.

It was not I, but rather my parents who decided to come to America. I was only around eighteen months old at the time. My parents wanted more opportunities and a better future for my two brothers and I. We came to the United States in 1969. I know it was not an easy decision because we were leaving behind a large extended family and substantial business interests.

Because I looked different than most of the other children and did not have an Anglo-sounding name, I was not always warmly accepted by my new American peers. In addition, my family and I missed our large extended family in Egypt a great deal. Fortunately, the inception of the St. Mark Coptic Orthodox Church in Jersey City in 1970 brought us together with many other Copts.

As a child, my happiest moments came when I felt like I was living in my own little bubble—in a cocoon. Everyone around me spoke English, yet in our house, we only spoke Arabic (my parents' rules). The neighborhood children were having hot dogs and pizza for dinner while my foods of choice were *molokhiya* and *kishk*. While most children of immigration might have been struggling with the cultural elements associated with such a transition, I actually felt a greater need to cling to my Egyptian identity. My happiest memory as a young boy was leaving school every afternoon to find my beautiful, smiling mother standing outside the school gate, waiting to walk me back home. There was nothing more blissful or reassuring to me.

I would advise any newcomer to the United States to first find a Coptic Church in their area, and then find a residence near the church. Be very selective in the advice you choose to follow, for many will volunteer advice. The steps you take at the very beginning will be the most important in determining the direction of your future. For people who are considering immigration to the United States today, you should have some kind of employment already set up, or at least have a well-developed game plan for the future, prior to making the move.

The homesickness element of new immigrants is not as crippling today due to technology, Skype, Facebook, the Internet, etc. Also, immigrants nowadays have a much larger support network due to the numerous Coptic Churches in the United States, and the large gathering of Copts around those churches. Finally, there are more resources and opportunities available to immigrants now than there ever was in the late 1960's.

Many Copts who are now well established as legal professionals are all too happy to provide advice and help to new immigrants on a pro bono basis. Such help includes answering all kinds of legal questions, assistance in filing out immigration forms, aid in forming a new business, and providing various other legal services.

The churches are always more than eager to offer assistance and give as much guidance as possible to new immigrants. Because the priest is typically the first point of contact for a new immigrant, he can appropriately guide the new immigrant to those who can help with housing, schooling, employment, legal and medical issues, and the like. Churches should consider forming a "New Immigrant Committee" to handle these matters on a regular basis.

Mrs. Mervat E.

I grew up seeing my father who was a very educated man unable to reach his full potential because he was a Christian and was very stressed about the inequality of opportunities for Christians in Egypt. That is why I decided to come to America. It was an easy decision for me because I was young and had no fears. I also did not have any children yet when I came to the United States.

I did not have any good experiences in the first two years. The hardest experience during this time was being homesick and unable to see my family. My living standards were much less than what I had in Egypt. My advice for newcomers is that they work diligently to reach their dreams. Do not wait for things to come to you. I would advise people who are considering immigration to the United States to be prepared to work hard. In addition, do not only just trust Egyptians. Some people may not have your best interests at heart.

The difference now for new immigrants is that there are many Coptic Churches everywhere. When I first came to the United States, there were only two Coptic Churches in all of America. I think newcomers have that advantage now because many churches are doing more than enough to help the new arrivals from Egypt establish residencies and integrate into their church communities.

Chapter 4

How Copts Adapted to the New Culture

> "And do not be conformed to this world, but be transformed by the renewing of your mind, that you may prove what is that good and acceptable and perfect will of God."
>
> Romans 12:2

Culture consists of socially acquired information through beliefs, values, knowledge, and ideas. Culture impacts the behavior and the attitude of the person and especially in the family setting, as well as each individual's spirituality and relationship with God. The change from a familiar environment, which I call our "home culture," to an unfamiliar culture, which is the "host culture" for many Christian Egyptian-Americans, is a challenging one. By the grace of God, this chapter addresses how Coptic Christians adapt to this new culture. In addition, illustration of some of the challenges that face the Coptic Christians in America are also discussed and brought to light to expound on the impact of the adaptation required by the family within the family relationships and also on their spirituality and relationship with God.

Why Immigration?

People actually emigrate from one culture to another culture for several reasons. A culture is composed of the beliefs, social norms, and material traits of a social group. Ordinarily, people who live in the same culture share attitudes, values, principles, goals, and practices together. Culture is something in which we are immersed, and actually, we absorb from the culture, as if by osmosis, usually while we are unconscious of this process. We tend to accept cultural values—most of the time without thinking about them. When people emigrate from one culture to another culture, they definitely have to adapt to the new culture. The way to their adaptation has profound impact on many things, but the focus is predominantly on their spirituality and family relationships. There are several reasons that primarily the Christian Egyptians—the Copts—consider immigration to the United States.

Why Coptic Migration to the U.S.A.?

1. There are too many pressures back home in Egypt. Whether it is economic pressure, political pressure, or religious pressure, so many people are seeking freedom, seeking a country in which they can live their faith and enjoy their freedom, and seeking a life in a country like the United States.

2. Another reason people immigrated to the United States was to seek a better life. They emigrated from a developing country to a developed country in search for this better life—whether this better life is in education, or in careers, or in job opportunities. Some people came to the United States because their work transferred them to America. Maybe they did not consider immigration, but because of their work, they came to the United States. On a similar note, others may have come to the United States to pursue their studies.

3. Many people came to America because of circumstance. Some came because of marriage, having met their American spouses in Egypt and after marriage moved with them to the United States. Other people came through the immigration lottery. They applied to emigrate and they obtained it. Some people came to the United States for medi-

cal treatment. There are many families who have disabled children and they said they believed that America would be a better country to take care of their children.
4. Some people only considered immigration because their brothers or their sisters emigrated before them and they want to be reunited with their families. Their family applied for them and they obtained their Green Card.[12] Thus, they were able to move to the United States.
5. Some people like to travel to different countries and different continents. They may have come to visit America and loved this country. Thus, they considered moving here.
6. Some others were simply dissatisfied with their lives. That could be why they moved to the United States seeking satisfaction. They think that maybe if they move to another country or to another culture, they will find happiness.
7. Finally, there are some other Egyptians that immigrated to America for the purpose of service. There are many priests who came to the United States because the Church delegated them to serve the Coptic community in America.

---

[12] A Green Card is evidence of lawful permanent resident status in the United States.

Adaptation

Adaptation is the degree of change that occurs when individuals move from a familiar environment to an unfamiliar environment. How much change and what is the degree of change in one's personality is what determines adaptation and acculturation. Adaptation is a gradual process, in which the person is transformed to adapt to a new culture or environment. There are four stages of adaptation, and each stage will take time. It is not a process that happens overnight. Adaptation is influenced by many factors, including environmental factors, dynamics related to the host culture, and also individual expectations and motivation from the new culture.

When people confront a new culture and begin to interact and have contact within a new society, their interactions will cause conflict or a crisis between the dominant culture and the non-dominant culture. Because of this conflict or crisis, this actually further helps the person to adapt. In reality, adaptation happens to both groups. Not only does adaptation happen to the non-dominant group, but also to the dominant group because they also have to adapt and accomodate for the immigrants and the minorities who are coming to this culture.

Chapter 5

STAGES OF ADAPTATION

*"And let us not grow weary while doing good,
for in due season we shall reap if we do not lose heart."*

Galatians 6:9

Adaptation is part of human culture. Throughout one's life, adaptation to culture, persons, work environment, school experiences, and many other factors demand that one exercise the ability to adapt. Adaptation requires a certain measure of flexibility or otherwise, if the system is too rigid, it will break. There are fours stages of adaptation.

Honeymoon Stage
The first stage is the "honeymoon stage." For some

Egyptians, immigration is a dream. Many people in Egypt want to immigrate to the United States—looking for a better life. That is why obtaining a stamp of immigration on the passport, or securing a visa, is like the beginning of a honeymoon. Some immigrants believe that all their problems are now resolved and they will live a very happy life. The dream is fulfilled right now.

Hostility Stage
The second stage is called the "hostility stage." The language barrier, then the homesickness—longing for one's family, relatives, friends, neighborhood, and church—causes more stress. The career aspect further intensifies the overwhelming anxiety. An example of this kind of scenario is a physician who practiced medicine in Egypt and comes to find himself not even fit to be a technician in the United States. Furthermore, he has to take qualification exams and if his scores are acceptable, he can then apply for a medical residency program. After all that, they may say to him, "No, we actually prefer American graduates." Thus, he waits for years and years to obtain medical residency so he can practice his career. This is a big challenge for many professionals. During this time, many financial obligations mount and pose more challenges (e.g., learning how to wisely spend). For this reason, many newcomers spend many extra hours working just to cover their expenses.

Another challenge is family conflict. The family may be divided. Some family members may want to return to Egypt, while others choose to continue in America. This may cause family tensions and stress. The identity struggle further complicates the struggles of the new immigrant—*now, who is the foreigner?* I have noticed tremendous confusion about the concept of who is the foreigner? For example, many times while I am on my pastoral visits to pray at our Coptic churches, and American visitors attend, I am told by some members of the congregation, "Your Grace, there are foreigners here." I simply smile and respond, "*Who* is the foreigner here? *We* are the foreigners."

The other issue regarding the identity struggle is figuring out who we are? Are we Egyptians? Are we Americans? We find the children and youth saying, "We are Americans," but the parents adamantly respond, "We are Egyptians." Thus, even within the family there are different identities. This stage is perplexing for every family member and takes time to resolve. Unfortunately, some people remain stuck in this stage and continue the rest of their lives in this phase of hostility. They don't make the transition to the third stage, perhaps because they refuse to do so.

Humor Stage

The third stage is the "humor stage." Why do we call

it this? The humor stage happens after a person settles down, has career stability, secured a job, has a better understanding of oneself, has more insight about the culture, has a place to worship, adapts well with the culture, and is more relaxed. There is a level of comfort with the Americans in this new culture. How do you know that the person is relaxed? When there is no longer embarrassment to share with others one's cultural and language mistakes. "When I came to America, I did such and such and such," without feeling embarrassed. In the beginning, when one makes cultural or language mistakes, there is a natural feeling of awkwardness that is not easy to share with others. However, once one finds humor in these mistakes, then these embarrassing incidences can easily by shared with others with great humor. This stage demonstrates that the person is relaxed. When people reach this stage, they believe that they have completely adapted to their new culture and feel completely adjusted to their new society. The majority of the Egyptian immigrants who reach this humor stage nonetheless do not move on to the last stage—which is a very critical.

Home Stage

The last stage is the "home stage." The definition of home now expands to include the *host culture* and the *home culture*. Now, the immigrant no longer says, "We,

Egyptians, do such and such, but the Americans do so and so." As an immigrant or American citizen, I can identify myself as an Egyptian and also as an American. Actually, I develop a sense of belonging to this country. I will feel that America is also my country. It is not just a host country for me. This country is my country, as much as Egypt is also my country. My sense of belonging to these two cultures is the same. With this sense of belonging, my perception of my identity will now change, because I will perceive myself as Coptic-American. I am both American and also Egyptian. When one reaches this point, the individual will have a better understanding of diversity.

The apostle Paul says, "There is neither Greek nor Jew, circumcised nor uncircumcised, barbarian, Scythian, slave nor free, but Christ is all and in all" (Colossians 3:11). All of us are brothers and sisters. All of us are the children of Adam and Eve. That is why a person will go beyond discrimination. He will see everybody as his brother and his sister. Here is the beauty of this stage—*unity in diversity*. Although we are different, with different backgrounds, there is unity amongst all of us. The person at this stage develops a sense of patriotism for the new country. This individual will be active and interested, willing to participate in voting and will be interested in the affairs of this country. Unless the Coptic immigrants know about the home stage and are aware of this final stage—I can tell from my experience and communication with many, many people who have been here for twenty or thirty years, they will remain stuck at the humor stage and will not make it to the last and best stage.

Egyptian-Americans can be classified into four groups based on their attitude toward the host country, which is the United States, and the home country, which is Egypt. *Reference the table below as you proceed:*

Table 1: Attitude Toward Host Country and Home Country

ATTITUDE	Positive→Egypt	Negative→Egypt
Positive→USA	Integration	Assimilation
Negative→USA	Separation	Marginalization

Their attitude toward the United States can be either positive or negative and their attitude toward Egypt can be either positive or negative. If a person is extremely loyal to the United States but does not have this loyalty toward Egypt, but is rather angry with and lacking interest in the home country, we call this group **assimilationists**, because they assimilate culture within themselves, and they refuse and have no interest in their home culture.

The opposite of this group are the **separationalists**. These people are very loyal to their home culture, but they have negative attitudes and lack interest in their host country. Actually, if they became interested in American culture, they would feel guilty as if they are being disloyal to their home culture. Consequently, they separate and rather isolate themselves from American culture. Thus, they are referred to as **separationalists.** They live as if they are on an Egyptian island in the midst of America.

When I previously asked *"Why immigration,"* I said some people are dissatisfied. Wherever they go, they will be dissatisfied and unhappy. They will develop a negative attitude toward the United States as well as toward Egypt. This group is called **marginalists** because they choose to live on the margins of both cultures. They don't have any interest in either culture, whether American or Egyptian, or any culture at all.

The healthiest group possesses a positive attitude toward their American culture as well as toward their Egyptian culture. They integrate the best of the two cultures in themselves. This group is called the **integrationists**. They are composed of those who have actually moved to the last stage, which is the home stage. Those who made it to that stage feel that America and Egypt are both their home. Now, they can integrate the best of both cultures in themselves.

Comparisons among the Four Groups:

As has been explained, there are four types of immigrants: **Assimilationists, Separationalists, Marginalists, and Integrationists**. Each group faces different challenges. Sometimes they get stuck in situations where they are unable to progress due to their inflexibility and lack of desire to integrate their two cultures—the home culture and the host culture.

ATTITUDE	Positive→Egypt	Negative→Egypt
Positive→USA	Integration	Assimilation
Negative→USA	Separation	Marginalization

Assimilationists—When an individual does not wish to maintain his own Egyptian identity, and seeks daily interaction only with American culture, we call this assimilation. Actually, these assimilationists become more Americanized than the Americans themselves. This is most common amongst children of immigrants and the younger generation. The younger generation often says to their parents, "We are Americans, but you are Egyptian." They absorb everything from the culture, even the negatives. They do not discern how to absorb what is good and reject what is bad. They absorb everything, and are very critical concerning the Egyptian culture, often speaking very negatively about their culture of origin.

Separationalists—These are the opposite of assimilationists. There is immense value placed on holding onto one's culture of origin. These are parents who say to their children, "We are Egyptian and we will raise you Egyptian and this house will remain Egyptian." They emphasize on everything being Egyptian. At the same time, there is a wishful desire to avoid interaction with Americans—in their minds, with the *foreigners* in this culture. As I previously said, the house will turn into an Egyptian island in America. Just as the assimilationists are critical of Egypt, the separationalists, although they live here in America, are critical of the host culture—America. They persistently speak negatively about America, and they are skeptical of anything from this culture. They want to keep everything Egyptian. This group is more common among the adults.

Usually, when there is a conflict between parents and children, for example, when a father says to his son, "This is an Egyptian house and I want to raise you Egyptian," and the son replies to his father, "No, I am American; you cannot impose the Egyptian culture on me," and then, they come to me for advice to help resolve their issues regarding this matter, I draw a chart for them (like the table above). I say to each of them, "You are here ... and you are here, and now both of you need to make another migration. Each of you needs to migrate from here, and here, to there."

Actually, this tension that develops between parents and children can be resolved if both sides become integrationists instead of separationalists and assimilationists. So, when I draw this visual chart for them and they look at it, they begin to understand. Furthermore, I tell them, "Whether we are American or Egyptian, we are *Christians*. As Christians, we need to integrate the best of the American culture and the best of the Egyptian culture." This is how conflicts between parents and children regarding their identity—whether they are American or Egyptian—can be communicated, explained, and resolved. Therefore, it is vital to understand and know how we adapt to different cultures. This is very important and useful in resolving family tension and family conflict between parents and children regarding cultural identity.

Marginalists—When there is little interest in maintaining one's own culture or in sustaining relationships with other groups, whether Egyptians or Americans, this group of individuals are identified as marginalists. As previously explained, this is more common amongst the dissatisfied immigrants who are stuck in the hostility stage. They had a dream that once they would land in America, all their problems would be resolved. They had problems in Egypt, but then when they came to America, they realized they have problems here also. Thus, they will be dissatisfied again and remain in the hostility stage and become marginalists. They have no interest in either Egypt or America. Their identity tends to be very confused because they do not want to describe themselves as Egyptians, and they clearly refuse to describe themselves as Americans. They say, "I do not want to deal with Egyptians," and at the same time also say, "I don't want to deal with Americans." Marginalists will have a very confused identity. Many of them end up experimenting with drugs or having issues with the law. It is crucial for clergy, professors, teachers, or counselors, to learn how to intervene. It is our responsibility to help new immigrants by showing them how to integrate the best of the two cultures and how to help them progress from one stage to the next, until they reach the last stage, which is the secure home stage.

Integrationists—When there is interest, both in maintaining one's original culture, Egypt, and in daily interaction with the host culture, America, this group are integrationists. This is more common among those who moved to the home stage and keep the best of both cultures. There is truth and wisdom in the saying, *"Civilization is the integration of two cultures."* Integrationists tend to be very successful in their careers. In addition, this group contributes to the transformation of the home culture, as well as to the host culture. They are influential to their home culture and are also instrumental in the transformation of the host culture.

Chapter 6

ADDITIONAL CHALLENGES FACING IMMIGRANTS

> "My brethren, count it all joy when you fall into various trials,
> knowing that the testing of your faith produces patience.
> But let patience have its perfect work, that you may be
> perfect and complete, lacking nothing."
>
> James 1:2–4

There are many other challenges facing immigrants from Egypt to America, which are referred to as "collectivistic" and "individualistic" cultures, respectively. The American culture is interested more in the individual than in the group. Individualism promotes self-efficiency, individual responsibilities, and personal autonomy. For many Egyptians, the perception is that the American culture is an individualistic culture. Individualistic cultures refer to the broad value tendency of a culture in emphasizing the importance of the following:

- ➢ Individual identity over group identity
- ➢ Individual rights over group rights
- ➢ Individual needs over group needs

Collectivistic cultures promote relational interdependence, in-group harmony, and in-group collaborative spirit; and for many Egyptians, they perceive that the Egyptian culture is a collectivistic culture. For many Egyptians, this poses a dilemma. Emigrating from a collectivistic culture to an individualistic culture presents a quandary to the family structure and their interactions with each other. In Egypt, it is important to have the family together, to celebrate our feasts together, and to stay together. The teenager does not leave his house until marriage. Young adults also live with their parents until they get married. On the contrary, in the United States, if a young adult, at eighteen years of age, stayed at home with parents after reaching adulthood, some may think perhaps this young person needs to see a therapist to see what is wrong. These two completely different perceptions often cause major challenges for Egyptian immigrants. The collectivistic culture refers to the broad value tendencies of a culture in emphasizing the importance of the following:

> ➢ "We" identity over the "I" identity—the group
> ➢ Group rights over individual rights
> ➢ Group-oriented needs over individual wants and desires

Another challenge is the "Power Distance Dimension." This is the extent to which the least powerful members of an institution accept the power that is distributed unequally—as in the hierarchal family. The power of the parent is full authority over their children. However, in other families, the power is distributed equally among them. When a decision needs to be made, maybe they will take a vote, and perhaps the children will have the same voting power or the same influence as their parents.

Therefore, the culture can either be the "Small Power Distant Culture" or the "Large Power Distant Culture," based on how the power and the authority are disseminated. In the Small Power Distant Culture, the children can contradict their parents and can speak their own minds. They are expected to show self-initiative, learn verbal articulateness, and exercise persuasion. Parents and children work toward achieving a democratic family decision-making process. Egyptians generally perceive America as a Small Power Distant Culture.

On the other hand, in the Large Power Distant Culture, children are expected to obey their parents. The value of respect between unequal status members in the family is taught at a young age. Parents and grandparents assume the authority roles in the family decision-making process. Egyptians generally perceive Egypt as a Large Power Distant Culture. The problem surfaces when the parents are expecting respect, obedience, and compliance from their children, but the children who grow up in the United States feel they have equal power and should be part of the decision-making process. They believe they should be able to express their voice and their opinion freely, which can easily increase tensions in immigrant families.

Adaptation has a critical impact on the family. Different members of the family may adapt in dissimilar ways. The same family can be comprised of all four groups existing together: *assimilationists, separationalists, marginalists, and integrationists.*

This is how these people may have to interact together. The family system changes after immigration. There are many restrictions in Egypt, but here in the United States, there is a lot of freedom. Freedom versus restriction often makes the parents become even more strict and over-protective, which in many cases elicits resentfulness from their children. If parents did not learn the language of their host country well, they will have to rely on their children or their teenagers to be their mediators—their cultural mediators. Needless to say, a power shift will occur. The bar will shift from the parents to the children because the parents now have to rely on their children to get things done. An example of this is a father who wants to submit an application for a job, but cannot apply on his own. He needs to ask his children to do it for him. Thus, the power shift is evident.

Reports of perceived danger in the American environment also adds to the family's anxieties and tensions in the family. As previously mentioned concerning the usual tension between the assimilationists and the isolations or separationalists in the family—parents are usually the separationalists and the children or young adults are commonly the assimilationists. When people adapt in a wrong way like separationalists, or assimilationists, or marginalists, they are likely to develop problems like depression, despair, social withdrawal, familial isolation, conduct problems, hostility, anger, anxiety, drug abuse, eating disorders, and other psychological or emotional concerns. Many of these issues are present amongst the newcomers who did not adapt well to the new culture. Because of all these problematic situations, often conflict arises among family members,

Teaching immigrants about these stages and the different types of adaptation will help them to adapt in the proper way and to integrate the best of the two cultures. Diligent and appropriate education regarding the stages and a healthy kind of adaptation are crucial in helping the immigrants to not only be transformed, but also to contribute to the transformation of both cultures.

Chapter 7

ADAPTATION AND SPIRITUALITY

"For I know the thoughts that I think toward you, says the Lord,
thoughts of peace and not of evil, to give you a future and a hope."

Jeremiah 29:11

The most pivotal point is regarding adaptation and spirituality—adaptation's impact on one's spiritual life and one's relationship with God. Holy Scripture and Church history demonstrate that one of the constant struggles of Christianity is due to culture. One example is the Judiazers. This was the group of people who demanded that the Gentiles adapt to the Jewish culture. Tension between the Judiazers and the Gentiles arose (Galatians 1). Another example is what happened in the church at Corinth (Corinthians 6:9-10). There was a major culture clash between the Jews and the Greeks. A third example can be found in the Book of Acts, Chapter 17 between the Stoics and the Epicureans.

Clashing Cultural Trends

Humanism. Man is the measure of all things. He is the highest being. Man is god. That is humanism, as though they listened to what the serpent said to Eve in Genesis Chapter 3, "You shall be like God."

Materialism: Another trend is materialism. Acquisition of material goods is the ultimate goal for the person. For these individuals, money is god.

Hedonism. In the third group, hedonism (sensual pleasure) is the highest good. If it feels good, it is good. So in this case, pleasure is god.

So then, these three cultural trends can be summed up as follows:

>Man is god
>Money is god
>Pleasure is god

It is quite remarkable how many years ago St. Paul addressed these same challenges in his letter to Timothy and spoke about these three trends (2 Timothy 3:1–5):

"But know this, that in the last days perilous times will come: For men will be ...

1. *Lovers of themselves*—Humanism
2. *Lovers of money*—Materialism
3. *Lovers of pleasure*—Hedonism

... rather than lovers of God!"

Another alarming challenge is the inclination regarding different fields of study, such as in theology. Now, it is said that all religions are true and there are just different paths to God. In biology, there is the debate of evolution versus creation, and in psychology, there is self-actualization. Bible ethics teaches self-denial, but atheists teach moral relativism and that there is no absolute truth, but rather that all truth is relative.

Diversity and tolerance is another trend that is unusual for the Coptic immigrant. Of course, tolerance is needed as a person reaches the home stage and will feel that everyone is a brother and a sister. However, there is a big difference between tolerating people and tolerating wrong ideology, politics, political correctness, and world government.

These trends are actually threatening to many Coptic immigrants. They feel they are threats to their spirituality. Thus, their reactions move to one of the four different types of immigrants (as previously discussed).

In the same way, there are four possible responses to these adverse trends. Christians will usually respond to these trends by one of these four reactions:

1. **Isolate** completely from the American culture.
2. **Assimilate** completely into the American culture and eventually adopt these trends.
3. **Marginalize** themselves completely and attack the culture.
4. **Integrate** and transform the culture—the best way.

How then does one transform the culture? As previously mentioned, if an immigrant makes it to the home stage and becomes an integrationist, then the perception is that this is my country, and I will feel responsible for contributing to the transformation of this culture.

Three Steps for Transformation:
- Understand
- Discern
- Influence

Understand: Read what is written in Holy Scripture—1 Chronicles 12:32—regarding the son of Issachar who had good understanding of the times to know what Israel ought to do. We need to understand the culture. What is best? There are *many* good things in this culture. That is why we immigrated to the United States. We understand the strengths of this culture and we also understand its weaknesses. It is then by the grace of God that we can (and in fact this is an obligation) to help this culture and to serve it, so that our culture will also be transformed.

Let us explore some aspects of American culture, and ask yourself how we can understand and appreciate it:

Understanding American Culture:
- Personal control over the environment
- Personal responsibility
- Personal accountability
- Change seen as natural and positive in the American culture
- Time and its control—people in America respect time, punctuality—(Something that maybe does not exist in Egyptian culture).
- Equality and Fairness—Everybody is equal before the Lord, whether he is the president or a simple worker

Transforming the Culture:
- Individualism/Independence
- Self-Help/Initiative
- Competition
- Future Orientation
- Action/Work Orientation
- Informality (and we can see this all the time in how people like casual clothes)
- Directness/Openness/Honesty
- Practicality/Efficiency
- Materialism/Acquisitiveness

Discern: After one understands American culture, then one needs to discern what is right and what is good for one's spiritual growth and nourishment. Discernment is a virtue of spiritually mature people. It is important to discern when to say, "Yes, I can take these things, adopt these things, assimilate these values as a Christian, but these other values, I cannot." Discernment contributes to the transformation of a culture. The more spiritually mature a person is, the more that individual will be able to discern between good and evil, as St. Paul said in Hebrews 5:14:

> Solid food belongs to those who are of full age, that is, those who by reason of use have their senses exercised to discern both good and evil.

Influence: The final point is how to influence the culture in a positive way. The Lord Jesus Christ told us: "You are the light of the world. . . . Let your light so shine before men" (Matthew 5:14–16). Each person must realize that each one has a responsibility to transform the culture. The following commandment is meant for all of us: "I have set you as a light to the Gentiles, that you should be for salvation to the ends of the earth" (Acts: 13:47). That is what the Lord said to St. Paul, but actually, this is for everyone.

What then are the tools that God gave us to be able to transform our culture? These tools are Holy Scripture, the Church, and the writings and teachings of the early Church Fathers. We have many biblical examples about people who lived in different cultures, but they did not only adapt well to the culture, but were able to transform it—like Daniel when he lived in exile, Moses when he lived in Egypt, Noah, and Joseph, the son of Jacob. All these great people were able to influence their host cultures and to transform their own cultures.

I would like to conclude this chapter by a verse from 2 Corinthians 10:5:

> Casting down arguments and every high thing that exalts itself against the knowledge of God, bringing every thought into captivity to the obedience of Christ.

How does every thought and every value become captive to the obedience of Christ? This is discernment. In Colossians 2:8, St. Paul warned us:

> Beware lest anyone cheat you through philosophy and empty deceit, according to the tradition of men, according to the basic principles of the world, and not according to Christ.

Therefore it is either you who takes every thought captive to Christ or you yourself become the captive through philosophy, empty deception, according to the tradition of men, or according to the principles of the world, rather than according to Christ. The choice is yours—either take every thought captive to the obedience of Christ, or run the risk of being taken captive by false philosophies.

Chapter 8

THE COPTS TODAY IN AMERICA

"Be strong and of good courage; do not be afraid, nor be dismayed, for the Lord your God is with you wherever you go."

Joshua 1:9

Facebook, twitter, instagram, iPads, iPhones, iTunes, snapchat, and so much more has brought us to a new age. To keep up with social media trends, we use these same tools to expand our ministries, reach out to the Coptic community at large, and extend a warm invitation of evangelism and fellowship throughout the world. Coptic Reader, Coptic World, Livestream, YouTube, Aghapy TV,

Coptic TV [CTV], Christian Youth Channel [CYC], Logos, and many others, all have become a means to be more connected; we have it all by the grace of God and can apply it in the ministry.

Once upon a time, the word "Coptic" was alien to our host country. Curious people grimaced trying to pronounce the word and understand its meaning. "What is that?" "Is it like Greek?' "Are you Christian?" "Do you celebrate Ramadan?" "I didn't know there were Christians in Egypt!" These were the common questions and annotations made by our American neighbors, colleagues, and schoolmates. Strange it is that the only country other than Israel where the Lord Jesus Christ spent many years of His childhood (as mentioned in the Holy Gospel according to St. Matthew 2:13-23) would so easily be negated, while in many parts of the world, the mention of an apparition of a saint would turn that location into a shrine.

From the early 1990's until recent years, many newcomers entered the United States via a lottery system. Because of their legal entry, many of these new residents had work permits and could obtain employment with benefits. However, due to having a minimal education for some or language barriers for others, many sought communities where they clustered together to work for large establishments. Thus, many churches were quickly constructed to serve these communities. Cultural expectations and discipline practices needed to be addressed as they often varied dramatically from the home culture in Egypt to the host culture in America.

Following the bombing on New Year's Eve at the Saints Coptic Orthodox Church in Alexandria in the early hours of 2011, we see the beginning of awareness of Christianity in Egypt on the level of the ordinary American and the global community at large—and not just scholars who studied Egyptology. Global concerns for the protection of Christians in Egypt circulated in social media. Many Copts, now one or two generations removed from the early immigrants, began marches and demanding human rights. Egyptians in Egypt and throughout the world also participated in marches and other demonstrations throughout the world joined the efforts of demanding human rights and dignity of all persons in light of the newly evinced persecutions of Christians in Egypt.

President Mubarak, successor of President El-Sadat, was soon removed from office (after 30 years holding tightly to that position), and the United States had elected President Barack Obama, the first African-American president in the history of the United States. On the heels of these extraordinary events, other occurrences throughout the Middle East were fermenting. The Arab Spring began a series of revolutions throughout many Middle Eastern countries, starting with Tunis and eventually culminating in Egypt, and then on to other countries. Wearied by the lack of social and economic progress, the Egyptian people were demanding change. All Egyptians, Muslim and Christian, were demanding a better Egypt. During this turmoil, Copts all over the world were unified in prayer and fasting for the Church, their loved ones in Egypt, and all the Christians in Egypt who were subjected to more persecutions—but now it was a public spectacle witnessed by the world. Americans, Canadians, Europeans, Australians, Asians, Africans, and Middle Easterners, Christians, Muslims, Jews, and people of all faiths, rallied for human rights in Egypt.

Amidst the beginning of these astounding and unpredictable times, His Holiness Pope Shenouda III reposed in the Lord after forty years enthroned as the Patriarch of the Coptic Orthodox Church and the See of St. Mark. The Holy Synod fervently labored to follow the protocol of the election process of the future Pope of the Coptic Orthodox Church. A select group of candidates were announced. The number was then reduced through an election procedure; and then reduced again to five, and then to just three. The traditional altar lot following the Divine Liturgy on November 4, 2012 declared His Holiness Pope Tawadros II the 118th Pope and Patriarch of the See of St. Mark and the Church of Alexandria. His historic enthronement took place on November 18, 2012, and was attended by all the bishops and metropolitans of the Holy Synod of the Coptic Orthodox Church and many religious and political dignitaries from all over the world. During the vacancy of the papal seat, the Church was under the auspices of His Eminence, Metropolitan Pachomius, who led the Church admirably. With the latest advances at the fingertips of many, these historic moments were televised and broadcast in every social media venue available throughout the world.

On the secular platform, the first election in Egypt declared Mohammed Morsi, a member of the Islamic Brotherhood sect, as the first elected president. Christian and Muslim Egyptians who lived abroad were allowed to vote in the vicinity of their home residence for this historic election. Within one year of the election, an overwhelming number of Egyptians of both faiths took to the streets in protest demanding the impeachment and resignation of President Morsi. Devastating violence intensified against the Copts in Egypt and a rampage of terror and mass church burnings were witnessed on every news channel and in every social media throughout the world. Prayer was the only real defense. Through many political challenges and a period of unrest, a new election declared President Abdel Fattah el-Sisi, a general in the Egyptian Army, the new president of Egypt. Following the Arab Spring and the many protests at Tahrir[13] Square and other locations throughout Egypt, a new sense of patriotism has been progressively emerging.

Due to the recent drastic and sudden changes and for fear of a backlash of religious persecution and injustice, many Christians fled Egypt. Thus, a new population of residents began to arrive in droves. During and after the Arab Spring, new residents in masses began arriving to the United States. Some newcomers entered on tourist visas, some on student visas, and some on visas for medical purposes. For fear of returning to Egypt, especially for those who had experienced religious persecution, many sought legal counsel and declared asylum. Unfortunately, these individuals often did not have work privileges. Thus, the local Coptic churches have had to shoulder the responsibility of care and support for these individuals' and families' financial, educational, legal, and medical needs. These new residents are now struggling as they work through the four stages of immigration. It is our turn to mentor the new immigrants throughout the process of adaptation.

---

[13] Tahrir means, "liberation," a town-square in downtown Cairo.

Today, Copts have an identity. No longer is being "Coptic" an enigma requiring explanations of our origins or practices. More and more people are cognizant about the Copts with a better understanding and a deeper appreciation of our Coptic heritage. Currently, there are three established dioceses in the United States (founded in different years):

- 1993—Southern United States—Alabama, Arizona, Arkansas, Florida, Georgia, Louisiana, Mississippi, New Mexico, Oklahoma, Tennessee, Texas
- 1995—Los Angeles, Southern California, and Hawaii
- 2014—New England and New York

We are distinctly Christian and our practices are not just a list of do's and don'ts. Many of our American neighbors and colleagues have learned about our heritage simply and coincidentally by our names—uniquely Christian and often after Coptic saints. Many have become familiar with the celebrations of the Nativity and Resurrection Feasts, which are celebrated at different calendar dates than in the West. Fasting food (i.e., food which is permissible to eat during fasting periods [predominantly vegan, with the exception of fish during certain fasts]), has become more accepted as many in the West have realized the benefits of fasting as well as a vegan diet. Thus, fasting practices for spiritual purposes are now easier to understand. Thus, the awkwardness of being different—being Coptic—has become increasingly a blessing and an open door to evangelism.

Chapter 9

BEYOND THE HOME STAGE: TRANSFORMING AMERICAN CULTURE

"As each one has received a gift, minister it to one another, as good stewards of the manifold grace of God."

1 Peter 4:10

Establishing a Coptic identity in the United States has been the first and foremost challenge for Coptic-Americans. As I previously mentioned, most Americans were not aware that there were Christians at all in Egypt. Thus, the fundamental step in transforming the host culture is to transform the mentality of our existing home culture, and to edify our new friends with knowledge about our ancient spiritual heritage that has withstood time and toil, but yet, celebrates a spectacular legacy that lives on for all generations.

Throughout the United States, very few states have had major communities of Egyptian immigrants in mass clusters: New Jersey, Tennessee, and Michigan are among the most noted. Unfortunately, ethnic communities tend to perpetuate stereotypes, which may hinder the advancement of immigrants due to a preconceived public image. Teachers, potential employers, bankers, and many other professionals in a variety of industries may prejudge an applicant based on these unsubstantiated stereotypes. Forming clusters of ethnic communities can also hinder self-improvement. This happens with many other immigrants as well. There is no dire need to learn the English language if everything around you is dubbed in your native tongue. Thus, if there is no personal advancement, then one is stuck, awaiting another generation to live and fulfill their American dream. There will be little if any interaction with the host culture, which will produce an immigrant culture of separationalists—living on an Egyptian island in America.

New immigrants must pursue three critical immediate goals upon arrival and during the first year in America: (1) Evaluate educational credentials, diplomas, degrees, and transcripts; (2) Learn English; (3) Learn to drive. Thus, they can enjoy independence sooner and contribute to their families more effectively. The financial enterprise should not be the only focus, but the holistic family needs—spiritual, emotional, and physical—are of equal, if not greater importance. Thus, parental roles and leadership are crucial. If there is a need to borrow money from the church, plan to reimburse anyone who kindly lent you in your time of need. Cheerfully share discoveries of resources with others, so that they do not have to be burdened by ineffective strategies. Prepare yourself to give back to your community from the same kindnesses and mercies that God has shown you.

The first generation had mutual inexperience and lack of resources. Thus, they were able to form cohesion based on their similarities. Generally, they had ambition, but they did not seem to be intimidated or discouraged by those who have achieved success because they were all in the same stage of struggling towards their goals. Today's new immigrants are sometimes overwhelmed by the diversity and luxury they see abounding in the various churches and with some congregants. Thus, they are sometimes embarrassed to ask for help and to accept assistance from others. The roles of the priests include helping these new immigrants to settle and provide them with a support system. Everyone is called to assist the clergy in this endeavor for the aid of newcomers.

Some people likened America to a melting pot while others to a salad bowl. Actually, if all immigrants merely assimilated, then it would be a melting pot and a distinct identity of each culture would not be appreciated. In a caldron where all the ingredients blend together indiscriminately, each ingredient loses its appearance and its nutritional value escapes from the pressure. However, the alternative allegory of the salad bowl is more effective. In this scenario, all the ingredients abide together and can mix together, but each still maintains its original distinct flavor, texture, and nutritional value.

Once "home stage" is reached, one experiences a sense of relaxation and comfort. However, I remind you that your work is not yet finished. You are not just in a better place by coincidence or even by some of your own efforts, but God is to be greatly thanked for all your accomplishments. You now have more tools to begin your labors—*no, not at a job*, but at life. You already proved you have achieved success because you reached the home stage, but now, you have new obligations beyond home stage.

Do you remember where you were a few years back? Did you forget all the previous stages—the "honeymoon stage," "hostility stage," and "humor stage?" There are many other people still struggling in each of these stages. These are our brothers and sisters. They do not need handouts or gently worn clothing. They need empathy from someone who knows what it was like to crave it but find no compassion. They need kindheartedness from someone who walked in their shoes and can feel their pain. They need direction and inspiration from others who also once needed to find their way and be inspired. They need wisdom from someone who strived to seize it and learned by trial and error. They need empowerment and encouragement from someone who finally achieved and accomplished goals and aspirations. Are you available? Handouts can be given by anyone, but Christian love is priceless and is a personal gift of gratitude to God.

What can you do to help? Seek opportunities in your place of work. Are there internships or scholarships available? Can you help someone with a résumé and avoid the mistakes you made when you first wrote yours? Do you have some important interview tips that you can share? There are numerous paths in Christian services that one can and should pursue beyond the home stage? Again, as I previously stated, it is our responsibility, not only as clergy or servants, but also as Coptic-American citizens to help in the formation, education, and advancement of new Coptic Orthodox immigrants. If we are not part of the solution, then we are part of the problem. Thus, it is incumbent upon us to remain attentive, thoughtful, considerate, and diligent in providing Christian leadership and fellowship to our brothers and sisters so that they do not get stuck at different junctures in the earlier stages and suffer needlessly with diminished potential to move to the "home stage" and beyond.

A multicultural society with diverse religious practices and customs and interfaith tolerance can be a two-edged sword. Dating at sixteen was and still is unacceptable in our culture and religion. Intercultural marriages are accepted, interfaith marriages, never. On the one hand, a minority population like ours has potential to be easily integrated into American society; but on the other hand, we must also set boundaries on much of this outer freedom that may cause a disturbance to our spiritual formation. Faith and perseverance are the most important lessons learned throughout the Coptic immigration and adaptation experience. Each step in each phase is progress, unless we impede on that development and remain lodged short of improvement. Among the many lessons on the path of adaptation are humility, encouragement, hope, selflessness, and acceptance.

Chapter 10

THE FUTURE FOR AMERICAN COPTS & COPTIC AMERICANS

"Now, therefore, you are no longer strangers and foreigners, but fellow citizens with the saints and members of the household of God, having been built on the foundation of the apostles and prophets, Jesus Christ Himself being the chief cornerstone, in whom the whole building, being fitted together, grows into a holy temple in the Lord, in whom you also are being built together for a dwelling place of God in the Spirit."

Ephesians 2:19-22

Evangelism! If there is still any doubt about why immigration, consider the time when the gates of immigration opened. Until that time, the Copts' evangelism roots were stifled even within our home country. In only one of half of a century, six continents have bloomed and flourished with Coptic churches and services to every nation, whether of Egyptian heritage or the native culture of that country. In a way, this is a time of visitation of the Lord—not merely just for us as individuals, but His Church that has persevered under His love and protection for over 2000 years. The world needs to know about Him.

God is wonderfully above time. Add emigration of the Copts, which began in the twentieth century, to His many miracles. The time was perfect and the hearts were ready. Atheism has become the new antagonist to Christianity in the West. It was time for the faith that had been preserved for over two thousand years to come abroad to America. Thus, if immigrants were only content to have arrived to America, they are missing their true calling.

Adaptation, as has been discussed in the previous chapters, has many phases. However, spirituality has the potential to grow vertically or spiral downhill. Now, in the twenty-first century, we perceive our blessed Church as a twenty-one story building, rather than a widespread building with twenty-one quarters. Now that we have achieved the adaptation initiative, we have become a strong thread in the tapestry of the American textile of a multicultural society. In addition, we have the obligation to help educate, direct, and mentor new immigrants from Egypt. They face some of the same challenges, as did the early pioneers, and some new ones.

It is with great joy and gratitude that we are where we are today. In all the hardships associated with immigration and adaptation, there is no doubt that God has a greater plan. "For I know the thoughts that I think toward you, says the Lord, thoughts of peace and not of evil, to give you a future and a hope" (Jeremiah 29:11). There is a higher purpose to this experience than meets the eye. You don't need to be a priest, a preacher, a deacon, or a Sunday school servant to be productive in the ministry of evangelism. Sometimes, just your Coptic name elicits recognition that you are Christian. Live up to it.

Many Americans of diverse ethnic and religious backgrounds have supported the Copts especially in recent times when social media forced the world to witness the systematic abuse and blatant persecution of Coptic Christians in Egypt. So when you strike a conversation with a friend at school, students on college campuses, at work, with colleagues, in the neighborhood, even in a checkout line at the grocery store, or people just inadvertently learn that you are a Copt, the response is now commonly warm and friendly. Use this opportunity to share your faith. People want to say, "Yes, I know something about your culture and your religion," or "I know the Coptic Church is one of the oldest churches." It is wonderful to know that your place in this country is recognized and appreciated. You no longer need to hide or explain your identity at length. You have so many opportunities to share Coptic Orthodoxy and introduce everyone you meet to Christ through your Christian ethics and model of faith and perseverance.

"God Bless America"[14] is a lovely traditional song that is sung by many Americans at important events or special occasions. It should not be just a song, but a prayer of all her residents. We ask the Lord to bless America and Egypt—our homes—our very sweet homes entrusted to our care and beholden to care for us, sojourners in the world awaiting the return of our Lord Jesus Christ.

> "And these words which I command you today shall be in your heart. You shall teach them diligently to your children, and shall talk of them when you sit in your house, when you walk by the way, when you lie down, and when you rise up."
>
> Deuteronomy 6:6–7

---

[14] Patriotic American song for God's blessings and peace written by Irving Berlin in 1918 and revised in 1938.

Chapter 11

AMERICAN COPTS IN THE FUTURE OF THE COPTIC CHURCH OF ALEXANDRIA IN THE UNITED STATES

"Therefore if there is any consolation in Christ, if any comfort of love, if any fellowship of the Spirit, if any affection and mercy, fulfill my joy by being like-minded, having the same love, being of one accord, of one mind. Let nothing be done through selfish ambition or conceit, but in lowliness of mind let each esteem others better than himself."

Philippians 2:1–3

It is incumbent upon us to strive toward building the spiritual and religious future generations of American Copts. By faith and not just ethnic origins, this is now as it was and will be the Coptic

Church of Alexandria that was entrusted to the care of St. Mark the Evangelist. What can we learn from him and adopt in our future progress in America as a traditional church? Though he was not an Egyptian by nationality, he embraced the Egyptian culture and shed his blood as a consequence of his faith in Christ and his conviction to transform the Egyptian culture from their ignorance and vile pagan practices to a spiritually rich nation that has upheld the true faith for more than two thousand years. These two thousand years have been laden with ongoing persecutions in one form or another. Are we really free from persecution in America? You are probably thinking of terrorism plots, but that is the obvious visible form of persecution. There is a more awful form of intimidation and oppression. Do not think that the Coptic Church of Alexandria is free from persecution now that we are in America, *"the land of the free."*

The word Coptic originally referred to Egyptian Christians. The real title more accurately universally means the people or congregation of the Church of Alexandria. American Copts can be second, third, fourth, and so on generations of Egyptian Christians. American Copts can also be non-Egyptian by ethnic origins, but believers and converts in the Coptic Orthodox doctrine of the Church of Alexandria, and thus, are equally children of the Church. Therefore, we must be concerned for all our children and address the challenges facing American Copts and their future in the Church. Understanding these new challenges provides needed empathy for the youth and families struggling in our American society. American Copts do not live in the Coptic bubble on an imaginary Egyptian island in America. They are not familiar with that scenario and are not isolated from American customs and way of life. They are part of the American populace, but their adaptation struggles are in maintaining the spiritual component in the cultural spectrum of modern-day politically correct harassment and subjection to contradicting philosophies.

Though we grapple to conserve our heritage and deep seeded spiritual values, we must foster a livelihood in the future of the Coptic Church of Alexandria in America by equipping our youth and converts with confidence and a genuine sense of belonging to the American culture and having fellowship in the Orthodox faith without neglect of our wholesome religious traditions. The United States of America has many wonderful characteristics based on its original Christian foundation, but it also has many challenges, which are very different from experiences in Egypt. Subtle persecutions via atheism and tolerance of immorality are on the rise and extremely hazardous, as silent cancers are the most treacherous. The global community made up of all people, nations, tribes, and religions was horrified when they witnessed the martyrdom of twenty-one Copts in Libya at the hands of ISIS. Interestingly, one of the young men was originally from Chad, but accepted the faith and fate of martyrdom along with his brothers, the Copts. The world can clearly identify the face of this kind of persecution, brutality, terrorism, and injustice. What about the other unassuming deceptive face of persecution? These masked persecutions are under the guise of atheism, tolerance of immorality, same-sex marriages, polygamy, and other forms of unrighteousness before God that exists more here in America than in Egypt. We love all people, but as a Church, we have an obligation to state our concerns when our fellow citizens are in spiritual jeopardy. We advocate for the truth with love and not as a vigilante group of haters. Our churches must address all the cultural flaws and social deceptions in our new home country, America. This is not someone else's problem, but our own. How true and relevant to our contemporary culture are the prophetic words of Isaiah the prophet (Isaiah 5:20), "Woe to those who call evil good, and good evil; Who put darkness for light, and light for darkness; Who put bitter for sweet, and sweet for bitter!"

Chapter Eleven: American Copts in the Future of the Coptic Church

American Copts are far more culturally removed from Egypt as the primary home culture. In reality, English is the primary language in the homes of American Copts and parents and even grandparents may have no experience of having lived in Egypt at all as a home country. That does not negate the influence of the strong and steadfast spiritual contribution of Egypt as the motherland to the Coptic Church of Alexandria, now and forever. Nonetheless, from a practical perspective, it is not rational to impose cultural aspects on these future generations in America. We highly esteem our traditions, but are cognizant that our borders have been enlarged and we must adapt to these changes and bring everyone who is willing into the fold. The Coptic Orthodox Church is not an elitist religious institution. Everyone should be welcomed and diligent efforts should be made to convey the true faith and honorable worship as these teachings were delivered to the first Church by Christ Himself and carried out by His apostles and delivered to their successors, and their successors to the next generation of successors, and until the coming of our Lord Jesus Christ in His glory.

We love our Coptic hymns that burn with zeal in our hearts. Can you enjoy a hearty meal while your brother just looks on and can just imagine what the taste may be? Would you not want to have your brother share in the savor of your delight? Just as we translated many of our hymns into Greek or from Greek when Greek was the universal language in the early years of the Church and from which the Coptic borrowed letters to add to our alphabet, or into Arabic when the Arabic language was imposed upon us through various forms of persecution, we must make every effort to translate and perfect these new renditions for all ecclesiastical services and traditional hymns into English, in order to truly continue on the path of the evangelism spectrum and spiritual agenda for future generations to be a vibrant branch in the Church. What is the benefit to the Church if only a few people understand the meanings of the hymns and the rest are just listening to nothing more than pleasant sounds? Can beautiful melodies alone bring others and us to salvation or must we understand and apply the message in the lyrics and melody in order to make the words our own sweet prayer to God, and thus, proceed on the path of salvation and build a relationship with Him? Is this not what God admonished Ezekiel for?

> Indeed you are to them as a very lovely song of one who has a pleasant voice and can play well on an instrument; for they hear your words, but they do not do them (Ezekiel 33:32).

Praise is beautiful, and no one should feel alienated from God's splendor and worship. People should never walk out of church the same as when they came in. Church is the place for transformation. We must understand the explicit language, social innuendos, and practical application according to our American culture in order to be transformed. Our churches, clergy, and stewards must be prepared to do that by sincerely caring for all the people and the future of the Church.

www.ingramcontent.com/pod-product-compliance
Lightning Source LLC
Chambersburg PA
CBHW031402040426
42444CB00005B/388